DREAMHEALER 2

GUIDE TO SELF-EMPOWERMENT

ADAM

"You have the rest of your life to change your future."
-Adam

Additional copies can be purchased at:
www.dreamhealer.com

Copyright 2004 by DreamHealer

All rights reserved under International and PanAmerican Copyright Conventions. Published in 2004 by DreamHealer of Canada.

Canadian Cataloging in Publication Data
ISBN 0-9732748-1-6
Adam, 2004, DreamHealer 2 - Guide to Self-Empowerment
Printed and bound in Canada.
First Printing - November, 2004
All rights reserved.

The information contained in this book is not intended to be medical information. See your physician if you have a medical condition.

Cover design and images by: Ivan Rados
www.ivanrados.com
Book Edited by: Dr. Doris Lora, Ph.D.

Acknowledgements

Thank you Ivan Rados, the artist, for all the effort and dedication you have put into the art for this book. When we first discussed the images required, we soon came to the realization that some of them were too complex to explain in words. You suggested that I telepathically send images. I thought this might work because it is one of the techniques I use to help people in comas. I telepathically send them images of familiar people, places or things.

Your intuitive ability has enabled you to receive the information I sent you, and your extraordinary talent, creativity and true artistic vision have created images that closely resemble what I had envisioned.

Thanks Ivan, for enlightening me beyond my stick-man level of art.

Also many thanks to my editor, Dr. Doris Lora, who encouraged me throughout the making of this book.

Most of all, thanks to everyone whom I have had the pleasure of meeting when our paths have crossed....THANKS!

Adam

Foreword

By Dr. Lee Pulos Ph.D. ABPP

As a clinical psychologist, I have been fascinated by the softer edges of science – by the fleeting glimpses we get of strange happenings just below our surface of current understanding. One of the reasons for my interest in the non-ordinary is that part of my practice includes mind/body health issues and cancer counseling. Not all chronic health problems respond to western medicine and I have investigated other cross-cultural healing modalities as possible complementary resources. This included many years of study and investigation of healers from Brazil, West Africa, the Philippines, Mexico and India. Of the dozens of healers I have worked with, Adam stands heads and shoulders above the rest and I consider him to be one of the top two or three energy healers I have ever observed.

But there is much more to Adam than his extraordinary healing gifts. His bandwidths of the brain are much wider than most of us and he is apparently able to drop into what physicists refer to as the Zero Point Field where all information past, present and all possible futures are stored.

Adam's second book, **DreamHealer 2 - Guide to Self-Empowerment** blends ancient wisdom with current understanding of the body's systems and anatomy, especially with the use of his unprecedented rich and original imagery that he has developed. Even though I have written a best selling audio seminar

– **The Power of Visualization**, I found that Adam's imagery and mentalizations were far more effective and appropriate to the range of health issues described in his book. I now teach Adam's healing techniques to many of my patients and have incorporated them into my own daily self-healing meditations.

Most of Adam's extraordinary abilities can be referred to as paranormal or beyond our sensory domain. Perhaps – but I consider his work to be para-conceptual in that we do not yet have a paradigm to conceptualize the powerful reality of Adam's experiences that break the rules of our consensual reality. However, Adam does extend into the theoretical realms by incorporating the subtle energies and string theory of quantum physics with the cause and effect of our everyday Newtonian world.

Adam has repeatedly reinforced in both his books what spiritual masters and shamans – the technicians of the sacred - have been telling us for thousands of years; that each one of us has the ability and inner resources to heal ourselves. This also reminds me of a remark that a healer in one of the more distant provinces of Brazil once made to me;

"If you get better – it is your own fault."

I have spent many hours with Adam in his seminars and in private meetings with him and his parents. The thrust of our discussions has focused on trying to understand his vision of energetic interacting, not only in living tissue but in the quantum domain. Adam seems to possess an inner spiritual awareness that I have observed in the pre-eminent genuine healers.

What is especially exciting for me is that Adam, despite his already formidable gifts, is just at the beginning phase of his abilities. His insights and inner sensing are expanding and extending into new domains almost daily.

It has been a pleasure and powerful learning experience for me to meet and work with Adam. Not only do I recommend DreamHealer 1 and 2, but I am looking forward to his third book which promises to move into even higher octaves of consciousness.

Lee Pulos, Ph.D. ABPP
*Author of **Miracles and Other Realties** and **Beyond Hypnosis**.*

Introduction

By Dr. Doris Lora, Ph.D.

Do we carry within us all of the information we need for optimal health? "Yes," says "Adam," who has demonstrated a highly-developed ability to interact with a person's energy field (aura) and thereby evoke "the body's amazing self-healing mechanisms." And each one of us can do it. Adam's unequivocal theme here is Self-Empowerment."

"It's just physics," explains this remarkable eighteen-year-old author and energy healer, crediting one of his mentors, Apollo 14 astronaut and quantum physics researcher, Edgar Mitchell, with providing him with an explanatory framework for his healing abilities. The universe works in mysterious ways, organizing the matrices of millions of human choices to manifest to the world the gift of an extraordinary healer such as Adam.

Consider the steps that were necessary. First, there was a space program. Then Edgar Mitchell, Apollo 14 astronaut, was transformed by the deep knowing that we all are the "stuff of stars" and dedicates his life to teaching this "noetic" way of knowing through the founding of The Institute of Noetic Sciences (IONS). Then the celebrity space man and the handsome healer meet at a Vancouver meeting of IONS. Hearing Mitchell's talk on the quantum hologram as a possible mechanism by which humans intuitively access information from other dimensions,

Introduction

Adam excitedly sees uncanny similarities to what he experiences as a healer. Together with additional mentoring from Qi Gong experts and other reputable healers, Adam acquires renewed confidence and begins his remarkable odyssey of individual and group healings. Subsequently, he begins to share his gift with a larger audience with his autobiographical first book, **DreamHealer: His Name is Adam**, *and through his workshops on healing.*

Now, we are graced with a second book (and more to come) from this singularly-gifted young man. But what does Adam mean – "It's just physics"? The Vancouver teenager summarizes his interaction with the quantum field in his workshops and first book: "All particles are fundamentally connected to all other particles," he notes.

"All information and knowledge is available in the field of quantum information. Every physical object emits its own quantum hologram. I can instantly connect to a person's energy system, individually or in a group, by projecting his or her hologram in front of me. I 'go in' and give the person's body information through intentionality and then manipulate the energy – loosen blockages, zap tumors – so that the person can find the way back to a healthy state."

In his few short years as a practicing healer, Adam has been the conduit for hundreds of "miraculous" healings and personal transformations. Beginning with healing his mother of multiple sclerosis, then himself after a severe spinal injury from a fall, he broke into public awareness with his dramatic long-distance healing from inoperable pancreatic cancer of Canadian rock star, Ronnie Hawkins. In a recent follow-up phone interview from his home in Toronto, Rocker Hawkins said, "I am still cancer-free two years later. I can't explain it but I don't criticize what I don't understand."

In Canada, Adam's reputation spread rapidly. A cable talk show featured the high school healer and several individuals who had been healed. Consequently, the Vancouver teenager was inundated with requests.

With a heart as big as his luminous, dark chocolate eyes, Adam was "amazed and overwhelmed by all of the suffering in the world." He regretted having to turn down the parents of a 4-year-old with cancer because he had no time.

Feeling an urgent need to help more people, he reasoned that perhaps he could heal more than one person a time and discovered that group healings worked as well as individual treatments.

Furthermore, it made no difference if he was working long distance (nonlocally) from a photograph or sitting next to the person in the same room. Then as he matured as a healer, he began to understand more fully his healing role as a teacher and facilitator: that, in fact, we are all self-healers; we simply need a "guide to self-empowerment."

Adam and his family made themselves available to this writer for extensive interviews during two group-healing work-

---

shops in San Francisco and, subsequently, during the editing of this second book. In person, the young Adam evokes a sense of ancient mysteries, packaged in a winsome personality, wrapped around a pure, unspoiled spirit. Six-foot plus, slender, with olive-fair complexion and slightly-curly dark brown hair, he moves with the easy grace of the athlete he is. His open, direct gaze, friendly slight smile and natural reserve create a compelling charisma. In short, Adam is a "Babe." (Genius need not be nerdy.)

Adam has been able to see auras (the energy field surrounding all living things) for as long as he can remember, finding the childhood game of "Hide and Seek" boring because he could see the auras of kids hiding behind trees. His baby pictures show a noticeable "V" on his forehead. "I've been told it's the mark of a healer because it points to the third eye," he says, tapping the space between his eyebrows, "which is what allows me to see auras. It has faded a lot but shows up when I get emotional."

Adam's personable, typically-suburban parents were baffled and skeptical at first, yet cautiously supportive of their normal but atypical child. Observes Adam, "Fortunately my parents are rare and special spirits in that they came to accept my uniqueness and had the courage and wisdom to allow me to be me. For this I will always be grateful. Because of them, I have a better chance of reaching my potential."

Interacting with Adam and his family is indeed to experience delightfully-healthy family dynamics. Mother is outgoing, vivacious, fun-loving – clearly having fostered good communication with her two teens (Adam and his younger sister) and providing careful but non-intrusive supervision.

At workshops, one notes the enormous respect between father and son – father listening attentively to his son's words, always available to help with boundary decisions and facilitate workshop logistics – and Adam glancing over at his father for moral support when unusual questions arise.

This solid family support system helps to explain why Adam is, in other ways, such a normal, down-to-earth teenager. Unlike some individuals with highly-developed psychic abilities and rare talents, Adam is not eccentric, unbalanced, or out of touch with the practical routines of daily life: he plays tennis, he has a girlfriend, he goes out for pizza. Already at age eighteen, he has integrated his rare gift into a normal personality structure. His energy is such that people simply feel good, relaxed and comfortable around him.

Edgar Mitchell, scientist/astronaut-turned-mystic, describes his own personal experience with Adam and with the whole concept of energy healing – anecdotal, yes, but compelling support for his theories of quantum energy information. "The story of my life," says Mitchell, "is an account of being hit on the head with astonishing experiences, which drove me to find an explanation," hence his dedication to "fringe" topics such as the science of consciousness as well as more mainstream physics research.

Mitchell was healed "energetically" of prostate cancer several years ago in a "group healing ceremony" by IONS board members. Then, as if he needed anymore head-knockers, he was diagnosed with a carcinoma on the kidney in early December of 2003. Doctors wanted to operate, but he declined and called his young Canadian mentee instead.

Adam worked "nonlocally" with his astronaut friend's holographic image (projected in front of himself) for six months. Mitchell underwent no other treatments except his healthy diet, exercise regimen and meditation. After one month, a CT scan showed that the tumor was markedly reduced. This past June, six months later, the growth had disappeared.

"We are simply blinded by the limitations of our current scientific paradigm," observes the sixth man to walk on the moon. "The most parsimonious explanation for my recovery is Adam's energy-healing ability."

In these pages, Adam lets none of us off the hook regarding our own healing abilities. Our wellness is first and foremost our personal responsibility. Working with a healer is always a participatory process, a two-way street.

Similarly, he is intent on convincing us that we all are DreamHealers—in effect, working himself out of a job. His enthusiasm fuels our motivation towards "self-empowerment." His graphic step-by-step instructions show us how to activate the immune system and return body/mind/spirit to its natural balance and well-being.

Introduction

"Eventually we'll have a more complete scientific ex-planation of abilities such as Adam's [and our own]," Mitchell believes. "What we know so far about the subatomic realm and quantum holography is only the tip of the iceberg."

And scientist Mitchell offers a word of caution: "One must be discerning in this field of energy healing. But Adam is for real; there is no fraud or delusion here. If you're curious, look at the theories of the new physics, as well as the growing body of replicated studies on subtle energy effects. There is nothing to fear and a great deal to learn."

Doris Lora, Ph.D.
Life Journey Editions
Los Angeles, California
October, 2004

TABLE OF CONTENTS

1

The Journey Continues

The purpose of my first book, *DreamHealer*, was two-fold: to tell the story of the discovery of my healing ability and, more importantly, to help people understand that we all have the capacity to heal and be healed.

Soon after the publication of *DreamHealer*, I became aware that many people needed more information. Readers were enthusiastic but often puzzled. They expressed doubts about their own abilities to heal themselves. They peppered me with questions about how to heal.

This second book, *DreamHealer 2 - Guide to Self-Empowerment*, is an effort to answer that need. It also has a two-fold purpose: to provide detailed information on how each of us can heal ourselves and others and, as a result, to address the enormous need for healing on our planet. This book is a continuation of my first book, *DreamHealer*, which contains essential background information. So I highly recommend reading the first book in order to fully understand the material in this book, which is almost all new information.

Since the release of *DreamHealer*, I have been contacted by many knowledgeable and enlightened people with messages of encouragement and support. I also received thousands of emails from individuals in need of healing. Some contacts were desperate pleas for help from people who lacked a basic understanding or knowledge of the connection we all share. In this book, I speak at length about our connections with each other and with universal energy.

Many requests for healing have been heart wrenching beyond words. I have been confronted by people who are at the end of their rope and "willing to try anything." I have been asked to quit high school, friends and hobbies, to allow for more time to heal others. One fellow even suggested I sleep less. Even if I were healing 24/7, there would not be enough time to address all these needs. This book is a step in the direction of meeting that need.

As a healer, I must always be aware of how much energy I can give to others and how much to reserve for myself.

Consider this parable:

There was once a healer in New Zealand who became very famous. He had been an alcoholic but his life took a turn when he discovered his ability to heal. People came from far and wide seeking his help. There was always a line-up of people stretching from his front door far down the street. For several years, he gave to others all the help he possibly could, while sacrificing his own needs.

Then one day he collapsed under the awesome responsibility that healing brings with it. He took up drinking again as an escape route. He never healed again ....

Every healer knows this to be true; give of yourself, but ALWAYS save lots for yourself. Maintain your own life, your own interests and the space you need. In doing so, you can remain devoted to helping others.

It is clear that with a world population of approximately 6 billion, we need millions of healers. My goal is to teach as many people as possible, since everything we need to heal ourselves is already within us. We just need the tools to effectively tap into the mind/immune system connection and use it to heal. Teaching effective healing tools is the focus of *DreamHealer 2 - Guide to Self Empowerment*. With this book, I hope to assist in empowering millions of people to become self-healers.

HEALING IS A CHOICE

All healing is participatory, no matter what the modality. Even Western medicine accepts the idea that patients must be willing to improve their own health in order for that to happen.

Many people have been encouraged to leave all of the responsibility for their own wellness in someone else's hands, usually a medical authority. Each of us must realize that we ultimately choose every aspect of our health care. We are in charge. In this way, we become our own masters; we claim our birthright of total self-empowerment. At every turning point in life, there are decisions which we make ourselves. We define and create our own futures. Our wellness - physically, emotionally, and spiritually - is part of this creation.

It is our choice whether we smoke, drink, take drugs, worry, or place unnecessary stress or risk in our lives. Each lifestyle choice has consequences, but we ultimately make the decision. Generally, people want to remove themselves from the responsibility of their illnesses. They tend to pass that responsibility on to someone else, particularly to a healer such as myself. However, everyone must understand that healing themselves is ultimately their responsibility.

When people tell me that they will leave their healing in my hands, I have a serious discussion with them. I will not do a treatment on anyone who doesn't accept the participatory nature of healing. The healer does not do the healing directly. The healer simply creates an efficient connection in order to facilitate the healing.

We also have other choices which influence our health. We can choose to ignore our own energy systems or we can dedicate time to understanding them. A healthy energy flow pattern will help each of us. To achieve this, everyone should strive to maximize their potential. When you are being your best self, the positive energy will radiate out in waves of healing that will affect everyone and everything, well beyond your conscious awareness.

LESSONS FROM A FIRST NATIONS CULTURE

The Europeans conquered a medically advanced civilization in North America, the First Nations people. In this culture, people know how to use nature to heal the body. Many alternative healing methods ceased when these cultures were suppressed. The type of medicine that was practiced so effectively for thousands of years was virtually outlawed.

Because of my First Nations heritage, I had the privilege of being an invited healer at the Nekaneet First Nations International Healing Gathering held in Canada in the summer of 2003. First Nations elders and organizers demonstrated the incredible dedication and enormous effort that has kept their culture and way of life alive. I will never forget the powerful energy and emotion I felt at this gathering. The traditional healers were committed to helping anyone who needed healing. They spent long hours in the hot sun helping all who showed up, sharing their knowledge and healing skills.

First Nations people accept the reality of spirit and energy interconnectedness, which makes them a pleasure to work with. Visualizations and dreams are an integral part of their culture and have great meaning. We would do well to learn this connection to our inner power from our First Nations neighbors.

2

Accepting Responsibility

What is the most extensive untapped resource in modern medicine? It is the power of the patient to heal himself or herself. Millions of people put the responsibility of their personal health care in the hands of others. In many cases, the underlying cause is rarely dealt with.

I challenge you to take charge of your own health. Make sure that your lifestyle choices are healthy ones. Accept the primary responsibility for maintaining your own health. After all, no one is more interested in your health than you are. Learn about your own body and how to avoid illness.

Your best defense against illness is your own immune system working at its optimum level. What you think directly affects the efficiency of your immune system. Do your own research so you can make educated decisions about what is best for you. For instance, if you have a pancreatic problem, get an anatomy book and learn how the pancreas works, where it is located and what it looks like. Learn everything that you can about the pancreas. Then you can incorporate this knowledge into the visualizations I outline in this book, making them more realistic, effective and much easier to do.

SET NEW INTENTIONS TO COUNTER OLD HABITS.

Belief System for Self-Healing:

> *I can be well again (Possible)*
> *I will be well again (Probable)*
> *I am well again (Being well)*

Wellness involves looking carefully at lifestyle, attitudes and emotions. Those seeking better health must have a true desire to reach the goal of "Being well."

ROLE OF LIFESTYLE

It is essential to have the will power and discipline to change your lifestyle. In many cases of illness, the individual's lifestyle is a contributing factor. The first step to healing yourself is examining your lifestyle from a non-biased (objective) point of view. Recall everything that you did today that may have had a negative impact on your health. If you are having difficulty analyzing your lifestyle, ask a close friend or relative who knows you well. Ask them to tell you honestly how they think you could improve your lifestyle.

Think about the people you spend time with. Your environment has a huge effect on your health. When those around you observe your efforts to improve your own health, positive thoughts will radiate out from them. This in turn improves your immediate healing environment and your health in the long term.

It may be more difficult to see a negative lifestyle factor when it is "invisible" (such as stress), than a more obvious poor choice (such as smoking). Changing your lifestyle for the better can only have a positive impact, so it is essential to have the will power and discipline to make the necessary changes.

The approach to analyzing your lifestyle includes not only becoming aware of negative aspects that are causing problems, but focusing on those which will create a positive impact in your life. Make all of your choices healthy ones.

Decide what habits and practices you must change in your lifestyle and take the appropriate action to change them. Take control of this power that you have to change any unhealthy habits and consequently your life. This is only a fraction of the incredible potential of self-empowerment at your disposal.

I have received many emails from people seeking help who have lung-related diseases, only to learn that they are still smoking. If they cannot throw away the cigarettes, do they sincerely have the desire to get better and heal themselves?

It would be unwise to spend my time and energy helping someone who refuses to make lifestyle changes and continues the pattern or behavior that may have caused the problem in the first place. The desire to take positive steps for your health is the same desire that will empower you to get better. The healer points the body in the right direction for healing: it is YOU who must continue in that direction. It is your body, so take care of it. You are ultimately in charge.

ROLE OF ATTITUDES

The second step toward self-healing is creating a positive social environment that will enhance your healing ability. The attitudes of those around you have a huge effect on your well being. Therefore, not only must you change your habits, diet, and thought patterns, you must influence people around you to change their attitudes and be more positive. When you and all the people around you are thinking positively, you are creating a perfect healing environment and increasing the effectiveness of your healing process. Conversely, when people around you are always negative, their negative attitudes interfere with and counter your positive healing process.

Negativity is the most common attitude problem that people face today. Your positive outlook will guide you hand in hand with your physical recovery. Everyone must put his or her past difficulties behind them. The past is past; you cannot change it. You can only change your present, which impacts your future possibilities.

Imagine two people in the hospital with identical illnesses. One believes (and so is thinking) that he is getting better and should be home in a few days. The other believes his illness is going to be with him forever and he is thinking that he will probably never leave the hospital alive. Which one do you think will recover faster? The positive person of course. The power of thought cannot be over-estimated.

All thoughts and intentions radiate throughout the universe. Everything is connected to everything else because the universe is composed of only energy. Thought or intention is a form of energy; therefore, every intention you have radiates out forever, affecting everything in its path. It is like a ripple in a pond . Every molecule in the pond is affected to some degree by that ripple.

Start today by developing a positive outlook from this day forth. See the glass as being half full, not half empty. In any situation there is always hope. Be the optimist. This positive attitude is essential to the success of your healing.

It helps enormously to have a regular companion with you while doing the visualization techniques that are explained in the upcoming chapters. If someone close to you has the same common intention and visualization, then the effect of that intention will be greatly amplified.

Finally, cultivate an attitude of open-mindedness. Many people are skeptical of what they cannot perceive with their five senses. A well-known children's book states in its wisdom that everything important can be seen with the heart, which is of course invisible to the eyes. In this way, we must look beyond our familiar paradigms and keep an open mind regarding that which we cannot see.

"A closed mind can only be unlocked from the inside."
-Adam

Wellness involves an open, positive, responsible, and participatory attitude regarding one's own well-being.

An easy way to explain the participation required in any healing is the old parable about giving a man a fish versus teaching him to fish.

- *Give A Man A Fish, And You Feed Him For A Day.*
- *Teach A Man To Fish, And He Feeds Himself For Life.*
- *Teach Him How To Make A Fishing Rod, And He Will Teach His Children How To Make Them.*

GIVING A MAN A FISH is like the healer healing a person without any participation on the part of the healee. The expectation on the part of the healee can be referred to as the "magic wand syndrome." No participation is required. No change in lifestyle is expected and there is no need to reflect on how the illness occurred. A totally passive relationship is created. The healer provides what is needed and the healees give away the responsibility for their own health.

On the other hand, TEACHING A MAN TO FISH requires two-way participation, just as with healing. The healer gives instructions as to how to participate in one's own wellness. Both healer and healee understand that healing is a two-way process. The healer's responsibility is to examine the lifestyle, stress and emotional responses that led the person to this point and to suggest the necessary changes which will prevent a reoccurrence of health problems. It is understood that this is a lifetime challenge which requires constant attention in order to affect permanent change. A participatory relationship leads to lasting changes in health.

To expand the analogy, TEACHING A MAN HOW TO MAKE A FISHING ROD gives him a lifetime tool. Similarly, the healer teaches the healee the entire concept of self-healing and maintaining a state of wellness. Consequently, the healee achieves a state of complete self-empowerment. Total responsibility is with the healee as he/she handcrafts his/her own fishing rod or state of health. A creative process has been achieved.

Ideally, people should understand the dynamics of the healing process completely and so be able to improve the design themselves in order to maximize efficiency. He/she should know that the ability to recreate their reality lies within each and every one of us. Accessing this ability requires imagination and a sense of knowing this to be true based on personal experience.

When a total understanding of the healing modality is achieved, the healee is able to teach others. This should be the ultimate goal of both the healer and healee.

ROLE OF EMOTIONS

Emotional problems are generally very complex and, in many situations, they develop into physical problems. Often we let emotions dictate our subconscious intentions and, therefore, our own wellness. If you master the control of your emotions, you are in control of your own immune system and thus your own health.

To master our emotions, we should practice tuning into ourselves in order to understand what makes us tick. What more worthwhile endeavor could there possibly be in this lifetime than to develop a deeper appreciation of ourselves? We can start by being aware of what pushes our buttons. What situations drive us to distraction? What characteristics in others drive us crazy? What triggers our positive and negative emotional responses, which in turn flood our systems with energy? Only when we understand what makes us tick can we set out to control these reactions.

It has long been an established medical fact that emotions play a major role in the efficiency of our immune systems. Listen to what you tell yourself; notice what replays in your mind. Is this working toward your own good, or is it providing negative reinforcement? The good must be given every opportunity to flourish. What you don't need must not be given the strength and resources it needs to exist. You don't need it, so get rid of it.

Visualize cleaning your room and throwing out all of the old, unused stuff - broken items, parts of things that you no longer have a clue to their origin. Be very thorough and selective. Keep only what you need to help you achieve the goal of recreating your new positive reality.

This "house-cleaning of your past " is necessary for you to understand what you have experienced, how you have interpreted those experiences, and what emotional baggage needs to be addressed. It is like eliminating the junk emails from your computer. If you don't do this on a regular basis, your entire system slows down and becomes less efficient and eventually dysfunctional.

Habitual emotional responses are difficult to change. An established pattern creates a "tape-loop" in the mind, going around and around on the same circuit. Break the pattern and move on, as it is detrimental to your health. Understand that your happiness is not dependent on what happens TO YOU and AROUND YOU, but how you process things WITHIN YOU. Your emotions depend on what you think, and you control your thoughts.

Life is for learning. What better goal could we have than to learn as much about ourselves as we can in this lifetime? Through learning about how we react to various situations, we also develop the ability to relate to others in a more meaningful and compassionate way. This new state of awareness sends out ripples of positive energy. Our concept of self, or "me" becomes more connected to everyone and everything around us. Improving the energy balance of one person ultimately affects us all.

3

THE LIVING AURA

Every living organism emits an "energy field," which is visible to many people in the form of light. This energy field is commonly referred to as the aura. The aura is a reflection of the organism's intentions and its physical and emotional structure. This aura or energy field surrounds every living thing like a bubble of swirling colored waves. When functioning perfectly, there is a harmonious exchange of colors throughout the aura.

I know many of us are born with the ability to see auras because when I change the size of my aura in front of a baby, its eyes tend to follow the change. This ability just gets suppressed as we grow up. It is not something that is accepted in Western society, so over time people lose this ability, either consciously or not. With a little practice, we can retrain ourselves to see auras.

The auras around plants appear to be colorless, similar to heat waves shimmering and rising up from a hot summer road. With humans, emotions appear to influence change in the color of the aura. Intentions manipulate the shape of the aura, and the physical structure of the organism appears to influence the manner in which the energy flows.

A person's aura is like a fingerprint or genetic marker that uniquely identifies the individual. Twins can be genetically identical but their auras look completely different. In a state of perfect physical health, a person's aura looks like an ocean of colors flowing around the body, with smooth transitions from one color to another.

No two auras are alike. They differ in color, intensity, size, and shape. People are always interested in what color their auras are. However, I don't see the value of categorizing aura colors (red means this and blue means that). The important aspect is the dynamic, harmonious flow of energy.

THE AURA OF A HEALTHY BODY

The manner in which a person's energy flows outside and inside their body is a unique identifier of the individual. Some people have a translucent flowing energy near the surface of the body. Others have another brighter layer which contains colors of swirling energy. Some people have lots of colors in their auras and others have very little color. Some auras extend well beyond the body, and others barely extend beyond the physical body.

The same person's aura can appear very differently under different conditions, depending on the degree of emotional stress, for example.

These observations have taught me that the most important aspect of a person's aura is how it flows. Harmonious flow of one's energy defines one's health pattern. A splatter painting may contain exactly the same paint and materials as the Mona Lisa; the difference is in the pattern in which the materials are applied. A symphony warming up may contain all of the same notes as the music which follows; the difference is in which notes are played with others. Harmony or coherence, in these examples, is what distinguishes chaos from order.

As a problem begins to develop, the energy begins to lose this harmonious look. The energy in the aura near the problem becomes "stagnant." All the cells in a person's body are working in unison and share an interconnectedness to each other; therefore, a change in one cell affects all the others.

None of us has a perfectly healthy body. We all have something that causes breaks to show up in our auras, whether it is an old injury, an existing ailment, or a developing issue. Re-establishing this harmonious flow gives each of us a goal to constantly be working towards. Many people have the ability to see these auras with varying degrees of intensity and can easily determine where a problem exists in the body. In some cases, if the problem is not too deep, the healer can use hands-on therapy to redirect the energy flow back to its normal state.

When the problem is deeper within the body, I have to be able to see the body's inner energies to cause lasting change. I do this by connecting to the person using quantum holograms. This process is thoroughly explained in *DreamHealer*, Chapters 4 and 5, so I only touch on it briefly in this book.

The various subsets or layers of information are accessible by selecting different holograms. For example, I am able to see the nervous system, organs, muscular-skeletal system, and the energetic system. Selecting a particular body system is similar to looking at a computer screen. My thought or intention is the "click" on the screen which accesses the information that I need.

The external auric view of the physical body gives me a broad perspective and is a good indicator of general problems in the body. If I need more information on specific problems, I connect to the person so I can change the holographic view or zoom in for greater detail.

Think of this process as similar to an architect viewing blueprints of a proposed renovation. The existing building is physically in front of you, but the vision of the future or your goal or plan is what you must visualize in your mind's eye. Each different "future" view can be seen on the blueprint.

During a treatment, I redirect the energy flow on the hologram in accordance with the optimum state. The stages between this perfect vision and the present health situation require adjustment and time. The problem must be removed, just as in a renovation. Most importantly, you and the healer must keep the vision of the desired end result in your mind's eye.

Some of the holographic images I see are more useful than others in viewing certain problems, just as some blueprints reveal certain details more clearly than others. The electrical blueprint is needed for accessing certain information, while the floor plan is more useful for other aspects. All are needed in order to complete the renovation.

THE AURA OF ILLNESS

If someone has an illness or injury, I can see the problem inside the body as varying shades of green energy. This sluggish energy has lost its direction in accordance with the physical problem. I refer to these areas as energy blockages. With different visualization techniques, I can eliminate these energy blockages and return the body to a state of wellness. While I am doing this, my intuition usually allows me to pick up other related information, which may help me to redirect the person's energy more efficiently.

Many illnesses have specific appearances or signatures that define them. Fibromyalgia (FM) and chronic fatigue syndrome (CFS) show up as a hypersensitivity of the nerve endings, so I use the nervous system hologram to view these. Multiple sclerosis (MS) looks like grains of green sand which bubble up from the base of the spine and collect in the brain. Organs that have problems have a cloudy ring around them. Cancer has a unique, radiating, green glow to it. With experience, I am learning how to more effectively and efficiently do this specific energy work. Every healing is an ongoing learning experience.

The auras that I saw in my high school's crowded hallways were overwhelming. I sometimes needed my girlfriend to guide me along. I made the conscious decision to turn down the auras, as it was far too much information to process. Once again, trying something new was an amazing learning experience for me. After I consciously turned down the intensity of the auras I was seeing, I found that I received far more intuitive information than before. This basically saves me a step, as I don't need to interpret visual input, which I receive in the form of auras. I can bypass this step, and access the information directly.

Our pattern of wellness is like a coiled spring. If you pull the spring out and let it go, it will return to its original shape. It is quite flexible and forgiving. However, if you pull it too often, the spring eventually will stay in its stretched shape. Our objective should be to stretch that spring as infrequently as possible. By maintaining our health, we won't risk stretching ourselves beyond our limitations to rebound back to our healthy state.

The living aura can briefly be summarized in this way:

- *Auras are flowing energy which change color constantly.*
- *Every living thing has a unique aura.*
- *Auras vary in intensity to different people.*
- *An injury or illness shows up as a break in the aura.*
- *In perfect health the colors are bright and the flow is unimpeded and harmonious.*

ENERGY EXERCISES

The following exercises, related to your aura, are to develop your skills in feeling and seeing your own energy, and then bringing in universal energy.

1. FEEL YOUR ENERGY

- *Hold your hands about 5cm (two inches) apart palm to palm*
- *Push your hands towards one another without actually moving them (that is, visualize your hands pushing towards one another).*
- *Feel the resistance, similar to two like magnets repelling each other.*
- *Spread your hands varying distances apart and feel the same resistance again.*
- *Establish the threshold distance that your palms can be separated and you still feel your energy.*

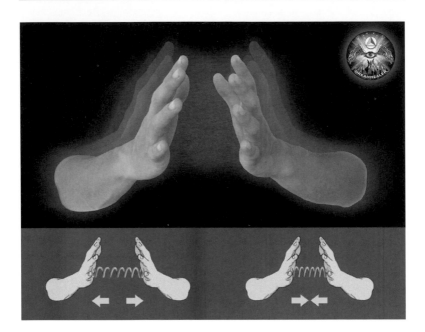

Feel your Energy

This illustrates how sensitive you currently are to your energy. With practice, you can increase this distance as you become more sensitive to energy.

2. SEE YOUR ENERGY (Images on next page)

- *Hold your hands in front of you with your fingertips pointing to the fingertips of the other hand about 5cm (two inches) apart against a dark background.*
- *Move your fingers up and down and in and out slowly. Think about the energy flowing from one fingertip to the other. Try this against backgrounds of different colors. With practice, the energy flow will look more defined.*

3. BRING IN UNIVERSAL ENERGY

- *Imagine all the energy of the universe being available for your use, circling above your head.*
- *Bring in energy through the top of your head and collect it in the heart area.*
- *Send the energy from the heart area down through your right arm, through your right fingertips and back into your left fingers and up through your left arm to the heart.*
- *Continue to imagine this flow as an energy circuit; from your heart to right arm, hand, fingertips, to fingertips, left arm to heart.*

At first you may see just a faint line. With practice, you will be surprised at how quickly you will see defined energy flow.

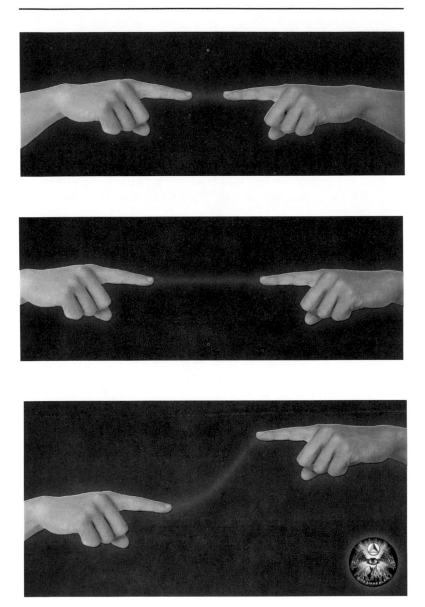

See your Energy

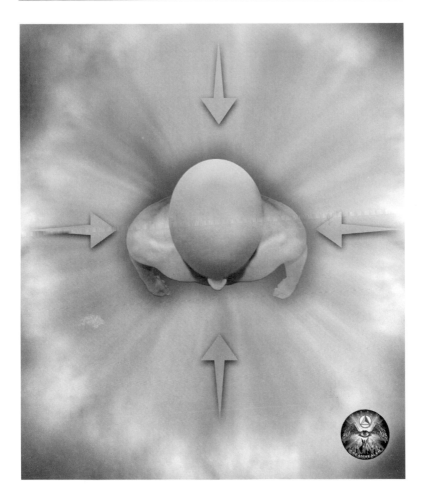

Bird's Eye View of Taking in Universal Energy

Look Past the Person to See the Aura

4, HOW TO SEE A PERSON'S AURA

- *Practice looking past the person.*
- *Concentrate on an area about 5cm (two inches) above the shoulders or head.*

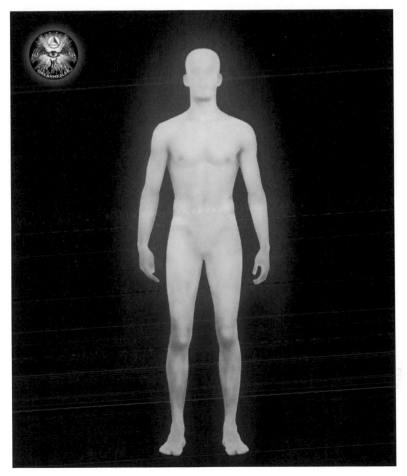

At First you May See a Slight Shimmering Aura

The aura may appear as a slight distortion. Generally it is far easier to see the aura after a treatment using the visualizions in this book. Practice makes perfect!!!

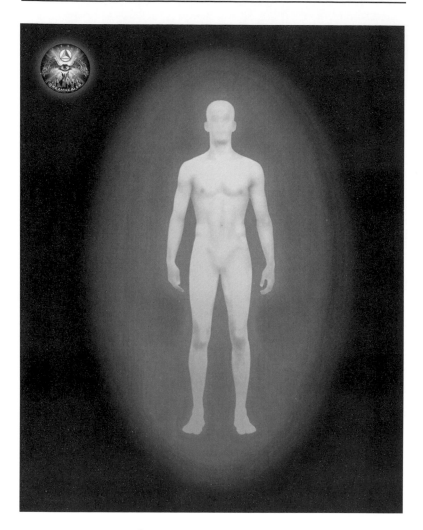

*With Practice you May See
Defined Flowing Colors*

Very few people can see the aura with the color intensity as in the above image. Keep practicing!!

5. ENERGY FLOW REPRESENTATION

A body without injury or illness has harmonious energy flow. A body developing an injury or illness has energy which is beginning to lose its path or direction. A body with a fully developed injury or illness has a break in the energy flow (can't find it's way back to a harmonious energy flow, or wellness). **This is an advanced exercise so keep it in mind as a long-term goal.**

Practice this exercise to see energy flow:

- *Stand in front of a full-length mirror.*
- *Relax your eyes.*
- *Practice seeing and feeling your own energy flow.*
- *Try both light and dark conditions.*

You can do this with another person as well, seeing each other's energy flow. At first, you may be guided primarily by intuition (feeling the energy). Soon you will be able to see it as well. As you develop this skill, you will find that your intuitive sense increases along with your healing ability.

TRUST THAT YOU CAN DO THIS!

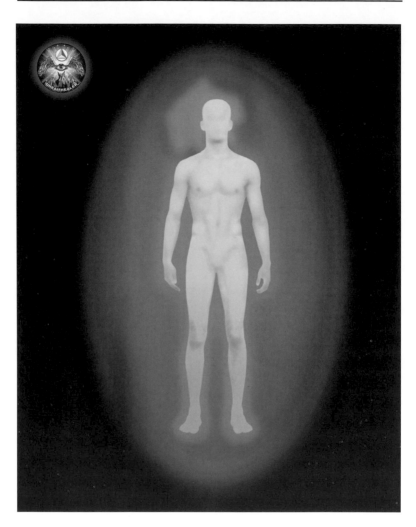

*Break in the Aura Which is Visible
in the Head Area*

4

Mind/Body Connection

IMMUNE SYSTEM

People tend to think of the mind and the immune system as two unrelated entities. You were born with an integral connection between the mind and the immune system as a natural self-defense mechanism. The mind directly influences the immune system. The mind is the command center.

When you are injured, your mind is subconsciously directing the immune system to heal the injured area. Your immune system responds by initiating various chemical reactions where needed. For instance, you don't have to think about healing a cut on your finger. It happens automatically.

Your goal in self-healing is to reach this same level of control over your immune system on a conscious level. Just as the body heals a simple cut, we all have that same ability and can learn to direct it consciously for more serious problems. There are an increasing number of medical studies confirming the mind's ability to control the immune system. This is the key to the process of self-healing and to maximizing its benefits.

From conception until the time of birth, each of us had a vital connection to another being as we all shared every necessity of life with our mothers while in the womb. This bond was our first experience of totally being at one with another physical person, where every breath of air, every bite of food, and every feeling is shared.

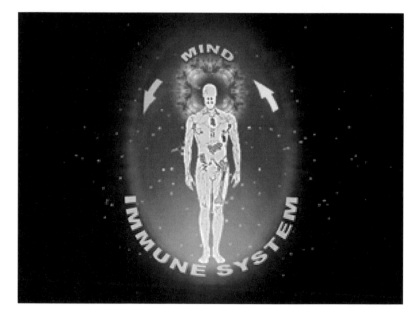

Your Mind Directly Affects your Immune System

AWARENESS OF CHILDREN

At birth, our own mind/body connection is complete. Every cell understands its connection to every other cell, and they function as one.

It is common knowledge that salamanders have the capacity to regenerate a severed limb. A medical fact that most people haven't heard of is that humans have some of this ability until the age of twelve years old. If a child has a finger cut off up to the first knuckle, the missing portion will regenerate within ninety days. The energetic patterns of our DNA mobilize to rebuild the missing part. What is even more amazing is that there is no scientific explanation for this occurrence. Surely this phenomenon warrants attention and investigation.

What we do know is that the genetic memory of the complete finger apparently still exists within one's energy field. Why is it that children are able to tap into this effectively until age twelve, and then the ability disappears? One reason may be that children's boundaries of "possible" and "impossible" are not yet well defined. For them, psychic and mystical experiences, extrasensory perception (ESP) and seeing auras are everyday events. These phenomena have just never been discussed.

I had the pleasure of doing workshops with kids at the International Healing Gathering in Saskatchewan, Canada. Most attendees were aboriginal, who have a cultural appreciation of our energetic connection. All were under 18 years of age. During the demonstrations to show energy, they all could clearly see it right away. One kid exclaimed, "Oh!...THAT'S WHAT THAT IS!!!" The others nodded in agreement. They had not yet been taught that seeing energy is impossible. They still experienced all events as equally valid.

Over time, this open state of mind and unlimited expectation is taught out of us. It is beyond the boundaries of our acceptable reality and is dismissed and not discussed. We are told there is a time and place for such science fiction notions and non reality-based possibilities, separate from everyday life.

Children expect nothing more in life than to experience everything to the fullest. They are excited about what each new day may bring and meet it with radiating self-confidence and a readiness to learn new things.

As we get older, we adopt the cultural view of ourselves as separate from everyone and everything else in the physical world. Our "ME " ideas develop. We are taught one set of expectations for our minds and another for our bodies. Our minds are supposed to achieve academic excellence at school. Our bodies are expected to grow strong independently of our minds.

Before I entered school, I thought that I was artistic. Then I met kids whose doodling looked like professional comic strips. My self-ranking plummeted. Every one of us has experienced this shattering of our self-confidence: it is vital to get this back.

At school and in our leisure time, we compete with each other mentally (academics) or physically (sports) in one realm or another. This is how we learn to view ourselves, and how others relate to us. We become known for our traits, such as the runner, the nerd, the loner, or the popular kid. We become labeled.

REINTEGRATION OF SELF

Society has placed perceived artificial boundaries on each of us. The fragmented self can be reversed so that we function as integrated beings. In reality, we are one with ourselves and one with everything. Our consciousness and the universal consciousness is an interconnection of constant information exchange. Some day a truth as obvious as this won't have to be seen as a self-revelation, but instead is readily accepted.

Subconscious and conscious thoughts should work together in order to achieve the same goal of wellness. The subconscious mind is molded by what we physically say and do and should be exclusively focused on the goal of maximizing wellness. This focus must be constantly reinforced.

Our subconscious thoughts and background self-talk are equally powerful for wellness and should be synchronized with the conscious mind. The conscious mind influences the subconscious mind and the subconscious mind is at one with the immune system. As a result, your conscious intentions have an effect on your immune system.

The most efficient way to direct the immune system through the mind is through visualizations at or near your sleep state. You are closest to your subconscious mind when you are sleeping, in a relaxed state, or in a meditative state.

When awake, make sure that you are constantly reinforc-
ing positive thoughts towards yourself and others - and towards
your future self - which you are now in the active state of rein-
venting. Think of this process as weeding the garden; only keep
what is helpful to you. If what you need flourishes, there is no
room for that which you don't need.

When I connect to a person's energy system, I resonate at
the frequency of that person in their subconscious healing state.
As a result, my treatments usually have a very strong impact on
the person's immune system. You can do the same within your
own body by understanding the important link between your immune system and your mind functioning as an integrated whole.
You have complete control over your conscious and even subconscious thoughts. Therefore you also have complete control
over your immune system and consequently your own health.

This thinking requires a paradigm shift. Not only does
Western medicine (allopathic medicine) view the body as separate from the mind and spirit, it also separates the body into its
anatomical parts according to the various medical specialties.
There is little or no awareness of the energy body. Every adult
needs to relearn what we once knew as children, but have forgotten: viewing the whole person as an energetic being is the key to
a state of wellness. We hold this key!!!

*Go with it. Explore it. Enjoy it. Move forward with
your new healing attitude.*

5

Healing Information

INTUITION

We all have the ability to heal, but not all of us have developed our healing skills. Learning these skills is like anything else we do; it just takes practice. Wayne Gretzky worked hard to be able to play incredible hockey. There is no doubt that he was born with a special ability that made it possible, but many athletes play great hockey. They just had to work a lot harder than Wayne, and even so, didn't achieve that level of excellence. Nonetheless, their hard work brought results.

In any athletic endeavor, the top athletes depend on intuition or feel. Perhaps they "feel" the energy shifts, but are unable to actually "see" them. Yet their awareness of intuitive abilities and being able to use this gift strategically separates the good athletes from the great ones in any sport. It can be called "anticipating" the opponent's move or "reading" the situation, or simply being "in the zone."

The same is true in business. All of the charts and graphs of an economic issue - the facts - must be interpreted in order to indicate a move forward or shape an executive decision. The process of interpretation necessitates the involvement of intuition, that is, how one "feels" about how events will evolve. Learning to trust your intuition and "go with it" takes practice. The same is true in every aspect of our lives. TRUST YOURSELF!!!

ENERGY CONNECTIONS

The universe is all energy, which is received and interpreted by us as information. This links all of us, as everyone affects everyone else. Ripples in the energy system are like ripples in a pond.

"All energy is connected; therefore, we are all connected "
-Adam

Can you imagine how powerful an influence it would be if all good news was automatically given front page status, and all negative occurrences were relegated to the back pages? Every morning we would awaken to an upbeat connection with each other. The positive intentions would ripple outward and reach everywhere. Don't you wonder why this seems like such a preposterous idea?

In order to explain the effects of intention and other concepts of energy healing, I discuss very basic principles of quantum physics in Chapter 7. At the quantum level, there is no difference between "here" and "there." In quantum physics, this is referred to as nonlocality. The effect we have on each other extends far beyond merely the direct physical contact that we experience with our five senses.

The study of quantum physics has only been around for a hundred years. There are many published reports and studies investigating the major role quantum physics plays in the energy field in which we live. However, the mere mention of the word "quantum" evokes a kind of mental block in our minds. Like mentioning the word calculus to high school students, we feel some anxiety. It's true that quantum physics is very complicated. But there are certain aspects of it (energy as information, for example) that can be explained so that everyone has some understanding of its role in our connectedness.

ENERGY AS INFORMATION

Every physical object emits information in the form of quantum data. We can pick up this information. The body's field of quantum information is accessed and assessed by the healer. The healer looks at the quantum information of the body in its current state. The healer notices the areas of difficulty. He or she then facilitates a change in the existing quantum hologram of the body by adding new information. The body's new goal is to update the physical to match the newly-accessed quantum information.

This is not as mysterious as it sounds. When we accurately perceive a common event such as who is at the door, or who is phoning, we are receiving nonlocal quantum data referred to as intuitive information. This ability can be developed further through practice. We often call this ability our "sixth sense." Some people have a very natural sixth sense for tuning into this nonlocal information system.

When I am doing a treatment, I project the three-dimensional image of the person in front of me and change the information through intention. This affects change at the information's source, which in this case is the person's physical body. It is this technique that I am teaching you in this instructional book.

We are all Healers!

In my first book, *DreamHealer*, I list seven steps to wellness which are a great start for anyone embarking on a healing journey. These should be referred to often and followed as closely as possible. (See *DreamHealer*, p. 154.)

The healing process involves telepathy, intuition and intention. Together, these abilities allow modifications to be made to the quantum information system of the body.

Telepathy is a form of communication using the transfer of images (thought) from one person to another. Once I am connected to an individual, I am able to check subconscious and conscious responses of the individual. Telepathy is especially useful for communicating with people in comas. I have had amazing results by sending images to those who can only express their ideas this way due to physical infirmity. In one case, I was contacted by the family of a man who had been in a coma for six months following brain surgery. I telepathically communicated with him when he was comatose, which awakened him out of this state. After two sessions he was responding to his surroundings and able to see.

Intuition (as I discussed earlier) is another quantum attribute used in the healing process. Intuition is knowing without necessarily having a rational explanation. Sometimes intuitive information is not easily understood logically, but it usually has something to do with the healing task at hand. One has to learn how to interpret the intuitive data received when one is healing. This information is integrally linked to the entire healing process.

Intention is one of the most important quantum tools. The intentions of both the healer and the healee are what makes things happen. Intention is the driving force that manipulates energy and information systems. When you have a large group of people all with the same intent to heal someone, their combined intentions produce amazing results. Prayer is one example of an intentional group activity. There have been many studies showing that prayer actually works. Even if only one individual has the ability to visualize his or her own intentions, results can be equally amazing.

The intentions of the person being healed must be sincere in order for any significant change to happen. It is not a question of whether people believe in prayer or distant healing. They do not have to believe; they just have to intend to get better.

Doctors face a dilemma when treating "terminally" ill patients, often feeling obligated to quote a specific amount of time remaining. This may not be a fault of the doctor. Patients themselves demand to know. The irony is that many patients are planning their death when they should be planning to regain their health. The mind is very powerful and one's situation is very much controlled by beliefs.

There is no such thing as false hope. New directions are always possible. When my first book appeared, many people who had been given a death sentence read the book. Deep inside, they knew I was not able to individually and personally help all of them, but they were comforted by being granted permission not to give up. They found new hope.

If we are all connected in life, then we are all connected after we leave our physical bodies. Death is an inevitable process which happens to every living creature. It is a journey we all have taken many times before and will continue to take. We cannot avoid it. What we CAN DO is improve our health and happiness while we are alive!

Don't get hung up on any one ritual of healing. It is not necessary to jump up and down, click your heels together three times, and repeat the phrase, "There's no place like home." Healing is simple, and everything you need for healing is within you anywhere and anytime. If it seems like there are too many rules, and it is more complicated than it should be, then you probably have made it so.

REMEMBER that YOU are ALWAYS the person in charge of your own wellness.

Another analogy: YOU ARE THE DRIVER of the car. YOU make all of the decisions - where you go, when you go there, and how fast you travel.

The healer is the navigator or map-reader, advising you on the easiest route to your destination and assisting as required. Many other people assist you such as the mechanic who keeps your car safe and the gas station attendant who provides you with fuel.

BUT YOU ARE ALWAYS THE DRIVER.
YOU ULTIMATELY HAVE TOTAL CONTROL

THE EVOLUTION OF SELF-HEALING

The wave of healing knowledge continues to build throughout the Western world. We have a long way to go, but people are beginning to understand and accept the fact that we are all connected to one another and to every living creature in this universe.

Notice how we are able to feel someone's sorrow or happiness. The entire world felt the pain of the victims of the 9/11 tragedy. A shiver went through my body when I saw the World Trade towers collapse. The sensations we felt were a result of our connection to one another. They are like ripples in the sea, which ultimately affects every molecule of water in the vast ocean. Our connection to one another is a vast pool of energy which extends in all directions throughout the universe.

It is difficult to grasp the concept of our interconnectedness because of the boundaries we create in our minds. These boundaries are an extension of our limited five senses. If we can't see smell, feel, hear, or taste something, then it most likely doesn't exist, or so we have been taught. In other words, if it can't currently be measured or explained through scientific study, then it isn't real. To go beyond these limitations would destabilize the very foundation of our current world view. Our entire physical existence is based on the concept of individual separateness.

Notice that we do accept as real some things not visible to the naked eye. We believe that electromagnetic waves are all around us, even though we cannot sense most of them. We believe in radio wave frequencies, yet we are unaware of their existence until we tune into a station. Everyone for the last hundred years has accepted the fact that radio waves exist. Accepting our own energy systems will be the next big step. It is just a matter of time before science can measure and understand this phenomenon.

6

Group Healing Evolution

In this chapter I will describe the evolution of my group healing abilities and the strategies I use in group healing workshops.

I receive thousands more requests for individual treatments than I am able to physically do. As I was trying to make sense of being given this healing gift, yet having a limited number of hours in a day to use it, I made an incredibly useful discovery: it is possible to merge the auras of two or more persons.

Every person's aura looks like a bubble of flowing energy which surrounds the physical body. While watching energy demonstrations, I could see the effect that one person's aura had on another. Given that this interaction exists, I wondered whether it was possible to merge several auras.

Also, I had always noticed in sports that the intention of

a movement preceded the actual motion. If a basketball player is thinking about a move in a particular direction, I can see a spike in his aura indicating this intention. Intention is both powerful and visible.

What would happen, I wondered, if I combined the intention and interaction of auras? I was eager to find out so I asked my family to help me with an experiment.

My mom, dad, and uncle were willing participants. I asked them to sit fairly close together so that their auras were touching. Although their auras still looked separate, they sort of stuck together when touching, as I had seen previously in large groups. Then I asked them to expand their auras by taking in energy from the universe. (I will describe this process in more detail later.) This allowed their auras to join through intention - like two bubbles in the bathtub that suddenly burst into one larger bubble.

THE MASTER HOLOGRAM

Once their auras merged, I was able to connect them collectively as one to the universal energy field, as explained in Chapter 7. Immediately, what I call a MASTER HOLOGRAM appeared before me. The master hologram contained and combined the information of everyone in the group. (I will discuss holograms in more detail throughout this book.)

Being pleased with the results of this experiment, I was eager to take it a step further. If it was possible to merge auras and manifest a master hologram, could the single master hologram allow information transfers to bring about positive changes to all present in a larger group?

In the past, I had helped several people with fibromyalgia, a chronic and painful condition. Presently there is no cure for it, so doctors typically prescribe large doses of painkillers. How would this master hologram work for a group of people with a similar ailment such as fibromyalgia?

It was easy to assemble a group of 12 people with fibromyalgia. Once their auras were merged as one, a master hologram appeared containing all of the health information combined. What I discovered was that the master hologram allowed for the transfer of the information to all who were united in a common aura. The information is transferred in the form of energy patterns, of which I am the conduit. By doing the same type of energy transfer treatment that I usually did for individuals, I was able to convey information to improve the health of all of the participants in a group.

This was a wonderful discovery for me and relieved the pressure of having to say no to so many requests because of lack of time and energy. In the fibromyalgia groups, most people noticed immediate and profound improvements to their health. Several participants stated that they no longer even have fibromyalgia. Their painful symptoms are gone.

These results opened the door to continued group treatments but I wanted to be sure I was on the right track. I emailed

Apollo 14 astronaut Edgar Mitchell (one of my physics mentors) for his opinion and feedback on this breakthrough. Here is his reply:

"Very interesting comments and effects. Regarding how it fits into the QH (quantum hologram) theory: although each individual has a separate and distinct holographic record, you seem to have helped them resonate with each other and with you as a group, almost like an athletic team that is "in the zone" and functioning as one. If they all have the same disease, then that disease has a distinct holographic pattern. Presumably, healing involves an inverse wave (or set of waves) to the pattern of the disease. It is interesting that you could have an effect on all just by focusing on the disease pattern. But, theoretically, no reason why not. Edgar "

Edgar has been an invaluable source of information throughout the development of my healing abilities and I always appreciate his input. His scientific explanations ring true to me. (For more information on quantum physics and how this relates to my healing methods, see *DreamHealer*, p. 51.)

HEALING IN THE PAST, PRESENT AND FUTURE

It was shortly after I began my work with group healing that I was invited to be one of the ten international healers at the First Nations International Healing Gathering I mentioned earlier. The Nekaneet people, who are part of the Cree Nation, hosted the event. What an honor it was to be there. At that gathering, I received solid confirmation regarding the success of a large group treatment.

Soon after our family's arrival, we were taken to the beautiful grasslands where the Nekaneet people have lived for many centuries. Ten teepees were set up in a "healing circle" with a fire pit in the center. I was given a choice of teepees. We had arrived fairly early so only one was already selected. It didn't take me long to choose one which backed onto a beautiful grove of trees. There was a constant breeze which picked up the sweet scent of grass.

Suddenly everyone was heading up the path to watch the youth riders approach on horseback. Between the rolling hills, a horse and rider could be seen in the distance. Soon there were more than twelve, all riding toward us. It was a magical sight, reminiscent of centuries past.

An eagle staff was held high by the leader of the procession. The riders were greeted by the elders, who are the link between the past and the future by way of teaching their knowledge. A ceremony to honor the riders commenced. It was an awesome scene. The next morning, the gathering opened with the traditional healing dance around the fire, accompanied by the sounds of singing and drumming. Then I started a day of healing in my teepee.

Culturally, First Nations people understand that energy is in and around everything that is alive. They are aware that it connects and influences everything. This connection with nature and its universal energy is held with the utmost respect. Everyone there understood the basis of what I was doing, which made my initiation easy.

They understood that the balancing of mind, body and spirit is what a healing journey is about. They were aware that spirit is the intuitive part of self. In addition, there was an overwhelming sense that being in such a beautiful setting was therapeutic in and of itself; it was the perfect spot for reflection. I also had the honor of working with several shaman and learned to understand more about their traditional ways.

With hundreds of people in line for treatments, I felt it was best to try group treatments. Prior to this, I had only done healings in groups with similar ailments. Nevertheless, I proceeded with varied groups. My teepee held twelve people comfortably, so I treated four groups of twelve per day, as well as a few individual healings. One lady in the group healing left without her cane. My dad found the cane after everyone had left. He ran out to give it to her, calling out, "I guess you don't need this anymore." Everyone in the area had a good laugh.

I also gave several talks to the native youth. These talks were always well attended. By the last day of the gathering there was a waiting list of over 300 people, so I decided to try something different. I asked permission of the elders to use the big outdoor tent for a large group healing. This was announced over the microphone and people showed up by the hundreds.

I looked at the crowd which filled the tent and realized that this was not a manageable number with so many people who were unfamiliar with the concept of grounding their energy. I asked that only the first two rows (85 people) participate in the healing. Everyone else had to move well back in order not to interfere with the energy of the participating group.

The results were fascinating - to me and to everyone else. We all felt that a powerful healing connection had been made.

It was interesting that the visions people received during the healing had a common theme - which seemed to flow from person to person. A man in the center said that he saw very vividly an eagle soaring with outstretched wings and wind in its feathers. On either side of him, others also saw feathers and felt wind on their backs. This vision gradually changed to a strong wind blowing from behind. It was incredible how people connected to one another in this state. Many were in tears from feeling overwhelmed by the energy in the tent. This was a fabulous learning experience for me. Out of necessity, I had discovered that many people collectively could take part in a group treatment.

STEPS IN GROUP HEALING

Since I have come to the realization that group treatments are possible, I have held numerous group workshops across North America. My intention is to help as many people as I possibly can and in the process I am continually learning more about my abilities.

The main point that I emphasize in these workshops is that everyone does have the ability to improve their own health. Specifically, I do these workshops to help you manage your own health issues, not to solve your problems for you. The "group" aspect of treatment provides a strong energy connection which enhances your own healing ability. After you experience this connection, healing yourself becomes easier.

In the workshops I explain everything as simply as possible and report everything exactly as I see it. The workshop provides scientific explanations and simple analogies for the healing phenomenon, which allows everyone to acquire a general understanding of the healing process.

Just as my abilities are evolving, so are the workshops. My first workshop had only 12 participants. Now each workshop generally numbers over 200. The combined and focused energy of these group sessions is very powerful. Because I still get many requests for individual treatments, I continually remind people not to underestimate the power of group treatments.

The workshops have proven to be an excellent step toward wellness for many people. Currently, each workshop has two group treatments from which everyone can benefit whether they have an immediate health concern or not. For people who are very sensitive to subtle energy, one group treatment may be all they need to return to their state of wellness. During these group sessions, attendees experience what it feels like to connect to infinite healing energy, for which I act as a conduit.

Once people feel this connection, they are able to return to it more readily and easily on their own in order to continue with their own self-healing. It is like riding a bike. Once we master what seems to be an impossible balancing act, we gain an unforgettable lifelong skill.

The first step is to ground your energy to expand your aura.

Visualize tree roots branching out of your feet. They branch down to more roots until the entire energy of the earth is engulfed in your roots.

On inhalation, pull the Earth's infinite energy into yourself from these roots through your feet. Once you become super-saturated with this energy, your aura expands naturally, since merely having this intention will make it happen.

On exhalation, push the energy from your head down your body and out your feet, connecting with the Earth.

Another method of grounding is to imagine that you are in a vacuum. On inhalation, feel the energy of the entire universe being pulled into you. This will cause your aura to enlarge.

These energies are easily influenced by intention. With the simple intention of taking in excess energy, one can do exactly that: take in energy. Once you have become super-saturated with this energy, the only place that energy can go is out. As a result, the aura expands.

Tree Root Visualization for Grounding

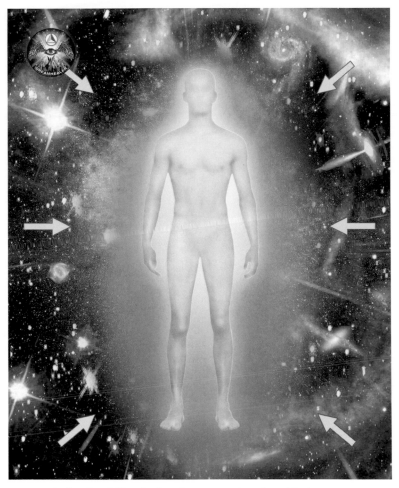

Inhale All of the Energy in the Universe

Pull the energy of the entire universe into you.
This will cause your aura to enlarge.

Your Expanded Aura

The second step is joining the auras of all participants as one.

When the aura is in this expanded state, it has the temporary ability to merge with other auras in the same expanded state. Now the group can join their auras as one.

Once you have allowed your aura to expand, shift your visualizing focus to connecting the auras, as shown in the series of images on the following pages.

Just as two bubbles in a bathtub merge into one larger bubble, visualize your aura merging with the auras of those around you until there are NO divisions between individuals, as shown in the images on the following pages.

A bird's eye view of the room would reveal one large aura filling the entire room. When people are close together, their auras "stick." They don't totally connect, but they adhere somewhat. If their energy is grounded and super energized, this adherence is more pronounced.

Now the group is merged as one. This is the same one-ness that is evident on a smaller scale within each of us. Your body is composed of trillions of cells, and every cell has its own unique and distinct aura. On a larger scale, they are all resonating harmoniously together to form your own complete and uniform aura. Just as the auras of all cells within us connect and work together for our own benefit, we can connect each of our auras to benefit all within the group.

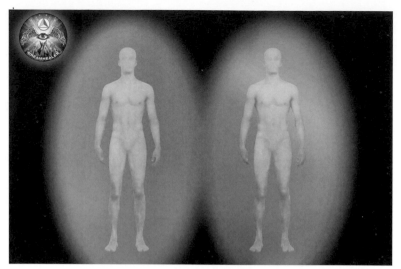

Auras Sticking

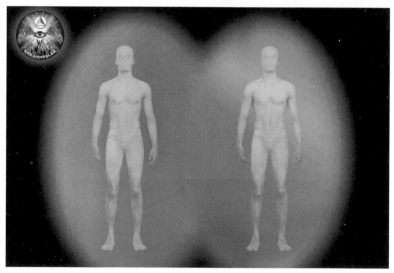

Auras Merging

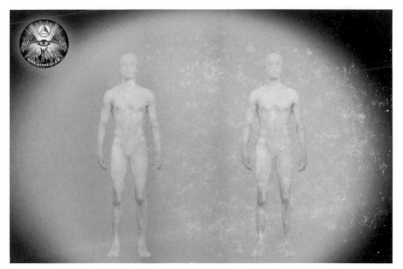

*Auras Joined as One Through Intention,
as in a Group Treatment*

Now what appears before me is what I call a "master hologram"- an image of a body with a collection of all the problems of the entire group. A change to the master hologram affects everyone in the group. In a group of several hundred people with random health issues, there is no way I can focus on every detail in the master hologram. What I can do is send as much energy through it as possible and, for many people, that is all that is needed to correct a problem.

When the master hologram appears before me, there is an intelligent communication of energy information. This enables me to receive and deliver healing information to where it is needed. For example, if I receive and send information about adjustments needed for a person's back pain, only those who need back healing information receive it. In each group, I address as many areas of the body as I can.

Simultaneously, people are doing their individual visualizations in the manner that I outline in the workshops. Everyone seems to know subconsciously where they need to send healing energy. Each individual knows best what he or she personally needs. This is not necessarily a conscious thought process, although people often come with a concern for a particular problem. I tell participants just to let it occur naturally, since energy healing is a natural process. Positive intentions can only bring positive results.

Group Treatment

A "Master Hologram" appears before me. Simultaneously people do their individual visualizations. It is very difficult to graphically portray or explain in words the images I see and work with. The image above gives a general idea of what I see energetically occurring during a group treatment.

The group process is very similar to an individual treatment. During any treatment, it appears that everything in the room goes dark and then I see a three-dimensional image or hologram in front of me. Next, the information appears before me in a format resembling a holographic computer screen. I can access the information in layers or subsets. I zoom in or out depending on what is needed to get the clearest and most helpful view. Then, with the energy of my focused intention, I can add or delete things to the hologram in order to initiate change. All of the information is in a form that I can manipulate with my intentions. (For more detail, see *DreamHealer*.)

What I am physically doing at this point is moving my arms, hands and fingers around. I only became aware of this after my Dad filmed me. This makes sense to me since we relate to verbal communication easier if our hands are involved. (Just watch people recall a story and see their hands move with it.)

During an individual treatment, I connect to the person by allowing myself to resonate at their frequency. In a group treatment, once everyone has merged their auras as one, I choose a person at random and connect to him or her, just as I would during an individual treatment. For a moment I see only that person's hologram. An instant later, I see the image branch down to include everyone in the group - that is, a master hologram emerges - which I then work with as I described above. This, in a nutshell, is the group healing process.

Everyone has a role to play in this participatory group healing experience. I act as the conduit for the energy and as a director/facilitator, by organizing and directing the energy to the location where it is needed. My primary role is to assist people in reaching the optimum resonance for accessing their health information. From this point, their own life energy takes over, and the information becomes intelligible to them. In this manner, I help people remember what they have forgotten. They become empowered to make positive changes in order to help themselves. The instruction to heal comes from you (your intentions), since your mind has the wisdom to heal your body.

At every workshop, the same question about energy arises. "If everyone joins auras, then won't I pick up other illnesses?" The answer is "No," it doesn't work that way. There is no negative energy. There is no positive energy either. It's just energy which is directed through our intentions. It makes no sense to give attributes like "good" or "bad" to energy since the only energy that moves is the energy that you intend to move. Keep every intention focused on healing and only positive results can occur.

Group healings are even more effective when everyone in the group has one common illness. When I adjust the master hologram for that specific illness, everyone in the group benefits more directly.

At the back of this book, I have placed some testimonials from participants at group workshops. In the future, I plan to do more group workshops made up of individuals with a common illness, as I find this is most effective.

7

Physics of Energy Healing

MATTER AS ENERGY

Einstein's most famous formula, $E=MC^2$, states that when you annihilate matter, you will get a certain amount of energy as a result. This proves that matter is simply compressed energy and therefore EVERYTHING in the universe is energy. Remember, when you throw a stone into a pond, every molecule in the pond is affected as a result of the ripple. Thoughts and intentions are a form of energy that radiate out from you affecting everything in the sea of energy, commonly referred to as the universe.

As we zoom into matter with a microscope, matter starts to look like Swiss cheese. The more we are able to zoom in, the more space there is between what formerly appeared to be solid matter. As magnification increases, solidity increasingly disappears and "space" expands. No matter how powerful the microscope, we will never find a solid piece of matter. If we did find solid matter, it would be of infinite density, and that is impossible. The bottom line is that everything and everyone is energy.

Once we realize that our bodies are all energy, we can appreciate the interconnectedness we have between every cell within us and between every living organism in the universe. Our thoughts, emotions, and mental and physical energies emit outward in all directions. They affect others around and close to us in positive and negative ways.

Quantum string theory states that matter is energy, which is a frequency or a vibration. Everything in the universe is made up of energies that vibrate at different frequencies and in different patterns.

Ill health is an imbalance of energy. Energy imbalance manifests itself in the form of different ailments, depending on where we develop an energy blockage. Energy blockages, frequently experienced first as stress, manifest differently from person to person. Some people are more prone to headaches, for example, and others to stomach aches when under stress. A communication breakdown occurs when our energy systems are not flowing in a harmonious pattern. What I refer to as our "pattern of wellness" is the result of our energy systems flowing in a harmonious pattern.

The goal of every cell is to communicate in harmony with every other cell. On a larger scale, it can be extrapolated that every living being wants to be in harmony and communicate effectively with every other being.

The science behind a group treatment is the merging of these energy systems (auras) into one large vibrating energy system. My part is tuning the group to a coherent frequency which makes this merging possible, like the orchestra conductor. Then everyone in the group is actually resonating at the same frequency, commonly called "getting in tune."

As a coherent energy pattern emerges, people feel this synergistic effect of resonating at the same frequency. Healing occurs when an energetic change or, more accurately, an information adjustment to one individual in the group causes that identical change to everyone in the group. I act as a conduit, connecting the group to this energetic change. During a group healing, all the individual auras are connected with NO divisions between individual auras.

Nature shows us examples of vibrating energies merging into one. Have you ever noticed that when a flock of birds is disturbed on the ground, they all fly away at the same time? Similarly, when you frighten a school of fish, they all turn away simultaneously as though connected to a common grid, and swim in the same direction. Every particle in their bodies is connected to every other particle. The impulse to move, originating in one fish, radiates outward in all directions instantaneously. An inaudible alarm bell has rung out a simple message to all.

Another force of nature not to be overlooked is water.

One drop of it is relatively powerless as a moving force, but lots of drops flowing together have reshaped our planet many times over. That's how group treatments work. The thoughts or intentions of many form the energy force which attracts and empowers the collective reality.

THE UNIVERSAL ENERGY FIELD (UEF)

We all tune into our different senses by picking up different energy frequencies. Our sensory system works like a radio tuner. Imagine the dial on a radio with words on it that trigger memories instead of numbers for stations. As you turn the dial, you tune into what you recall of that memory including sights, smells, sounds, tastes, and feelings. Everything we pick up with our sensory tuner is information from the Universal Energy Field (UEF). Everything that ever existed registers as information recorded in this field.

Every bit of information we conjure up in our minds is from the universal energy field. We all differ in our capacities to tap into this information. That is what makes us unique. Memory is the process of neurons in the brain forming and remembering patterns which help us connect to specific parts of the field.

To elaborate, when we come up with different thoughts, all we are doing is pulling the information out of the UEF. Then our minds organize, process, and interpret it so it has local meaning – that is, becomes meaningful to us in our physical reality. Of course some people are more adept than others at accessing this information, just as some people are naturally more athletic than others.

Not all information is perceived by our five senses. It is much more efficient to bypass this sensory level and go straight to just knowing. It is a little like cracking an egg. You don't have to crack an egg to know what is inside; you just know. That is because your brain has done some sort of processing that makes it unnecessary to crack the egg to find out what is inside. The brain's natural tendency is to process information in the most efficient way possible. Because of the interconnection we have with everything, the brain can use it's quantum processing ability to interpret information with maximum efficiency.

OUR ENERGY LINKS

Living organisms share a common energy that links them together. What appears to be "good" or "bad" energy is just energy behaving differently because it is at a different frequency or vibrational pattern. For this reason, it is inaccurate to give attributes such as "good " or "bad " to universal energy. As I mentioned earlier, no matter what vibrational energy pattern is operating in one's body, it is not transferable to another person's body unless both intend for it to be transferred in this manner.

If two or more people meditate together or join auras in a group treatment, their brain wave patterns become synchronized to the most orderly and coherent energy pattern in the group. This can be compared to the body's cells working in unison to form the body's aura.

DISTANT (Nonlocal) HEALING

Many people tend to think of distant healing as waving a magic wand. It just doesn't work that way. First of all, participation from both the healer and healee is required. The healer doesn't directly do the healing but simply directs the healee's immune system to the problem. This concept is explained at length in *DreamHealer*, page 57.

The science or the mechanism of the healer's contact is still not fully understood within quantum physics. Space and time – that is, going from point A to point B - has no meaning in the quantum world of energy connection. So, the healing connections do not "travel" so much as simply "register" instantaneously according to processes which we don't yet fully understand. What we do know is that the positive intentions of both people operate outside of conventional notions of time and space. There are no limits to what can be achieved by accessing the quantum realm.

In summary, many physicists now state that barriers separating us from each other are illusions. Understanding this is a step towards accepting that we are all connected. Then we will begin to see ourselves as part of an energy system that is connected to the entire universe.

8

Self-Healing Skills

Visualizations are concentrated or focused intentions in the form of mental images. A visualization directs your immune system to the problem and guides its action. Visualizations should be as close to reality as possible in order to more accurately direct your immune system.

In this chapter, I suggest ways to enhance your visualization skills, which will provide a solid foundation for increased self-empowerment. Practicing specific strategies such as fine-tuning, projecting a hologram and recalling details are skills which can be developed. Be sure to address general improvements in lifestyle and attitudes as touched on earlier. This is also an attainable goal.

FINE-TUNING

One of the most important requirements for healing is fine-tuning the ability to visualize - to see vivid images in your mind's eye. An intention regarding a cut would be simply for it to get better. A visualization can and should be much more specific. For example, visualize the entire healing process take place in your mind, step by step.

First, see the blood platelets clot the wound. Then imagine the entire healing process taking place until there is no doubt in your mind that it is complete and that you are better.

The most effective way to come up with suitable visualizations for yourself is to fully understand the problem that needs healing. Do your own research and learn as much about the illness and the anatomy of the injured area as you can. Because the mind is integrally linked to the immune system as described earlier, having the visualizations as anatomically correct as possible will more accurately direct the immune system towards the specific problem. Know what white blood cells look like so that when you visualize them attacking the problem, your visual image is closer to reality. This will help you guide your healing intentions more accurately to the source of the problem. Also explore the mental or emotional aspects of the issue. It is important to make use of every tool available to you on your healing journey.

The better you are at visualizing, the easier it will be for you to heal yourself and others. When you are visualizing, it is important to know that it is going to work. In other words, if you convince yourself that your body is being healed, then you will act on that belief by healing yourself.

Create a visualization. Continue practicing this visualization until you dream about it. Your body heals best when you are asleep or in a subconscious state. When you dream your visualizations, your body will naturally heal itself. In your dream state, you cannot distinguish between the visualization and reality; therefore, your visualization can become your reality.

Breathe energy into every cell. Every cell has a survival instinct and with this life purpose, it can and does communicate with other cells. The soul or total energetic body binds all cells into one functioning harmonious pattern of energy.

When using any visualization, remember to envision your youthful, healthy body. Your harmonious immune system is balanced and strong and you are resonating with it positively and confidently. REMEMBER that your visualizations are not limited to the boundaries of your five senses, but are limited only by your imagination (which is limitless).

PROJECTING A HOLOGRAM

An essential skill for healing yourself and others is the ability to project a mental image or a hologram in front of you.

When you use energy to heal someone, you must be able to mentally visualize that person. If you are planning to heal yourself, you can rely more heavily on doing this by FEEL, as you can do the visualizations directly on your physical body. You can also project your own image in front of you, or do both once you are comfortable with this concept. With practice, this becomes more natural. If you are not yet seeing this visualization clearly, just relax. With the constant intention of making this work, it will!

A hologram is a three-dimensional projection which contains all of the information (past, present and future) of that person, animal, place or thing. When doing healing on another person, this is extremely important to understand because their optimum state of wellness is within their hologram. This specific information is the difference between a simple image and a hologram. The two are not really interchangeable, but for instructional purposes, I use whichever word is easiest to understand in context.

When healing others at a distance, it is necessary to project an image in front of you. As a guideline, this image can be the person's full body form projected within a two-foot hologram. The size of the hologram is not crucial, as long as you can see the full body in your mind. You then see in your mind's eye the modifications needed on this image.

Many people find it helpful to have a photograph of the person they are working with, even if it is someone they know well. The photographic image, or a mirror image of yourself, is what you use as a BASE for your visualizations. Start with this simple two-dimensional image, and with practice and intuition, this data base expands with intelligent information. Eventually you will get to a comfort zone, where with practice, a connection to the person's quantum information, or quantum hologram, appears.

Trust yourself and your positive intentions. Intentions and thoughts are natural forces of nature - like gravity. Once you are able to visualize a person's holographic image in front of you, the next step is to use your intention (along with their participatory intentions) to assist them with their healing.

Concentrate on the injured area. Visualize the problem being resolved in the hologram, At that moment it is literally being adjusted in the person's physical body. KNOW that this is happening.

Use your hands and arms to manipulate the thoughts and energies as you see best. Be sure that after you remove the energy blockages or unhealthy cells, you dispose of them into space. Remember that energy is dispersed according to your intentions. Create your own visualization of throwing unwanted material into a vacuum, garbage or black hole. Without a host organism, it dissipates instantly. Use your best intentions to achieve a state of wellness in the healee, and also to maintain your own health.

RECALLING DETAILS

Have you ever thought about how you think? Think about it: How do you think? Do you think in images? Do you think in terms of your own voice narrating events and thoughts throughout the day?

Imagine that someone has the ability to read every single thought in your mind. This is called telepathy. Would the transition from one thought to another make sense to anybody but yourself?

Pictures or images convey richer and more accurate information than thoughts. "A picture is worth a thousand words." I refer to speech as "crude acoustical communication", as there is so much room for misinterpretation of words. We have all experienced such misunderstandings.

Telepathy is easier with animals than it is with people because the transition from one image to another is very simple and logical. My cat, for example, appears to have only about three images: food, sleep, litter box. That's pretty straightforward.

How vivid are the images you create in your mind? In order to learn to visualize more effectively, practice thinking in detailed images. Try staring at an image for 30 seconds and really burn it into your mind's eye. Would someone watching your mental image right now be able to tell what it is? For most people, it is very difficult to create vivid images in their minds.

To improve your visualization skills, learn to think in graphic images rather than verbal thoughts. Changing our habits from thinking in words to thinking in images takes practice. It is like any other physical training we do; practice makes perfect!

Disciplined mental training is required. People who have a photographic memory will most likely have an easier time, but anyone can train themselves to remember more visual details. Concentrate on every little detail about a person. Remember their eye color, wrinkles, scars, shape of the nose, hairstyle and any other outstanding features. The more you practice this, the more natural and habitual it will become.

You could also practice looking at pictures of people and try to fix their facial images in your mind. A way to form an image of yourself in your mind is to stand in front of a mirror; then close your eyes and recall what you look like.

An easy beginning exercise is to visualize people you know when talking to them on the phone. Picture them in greater detail every time you speak to them. Build an image of them in your mind's eye. Make it a habit. You will find that it gets easier with practice. This will prove to you that YOU CAN DO IT!!!

A lady approached me after a workshop saying that she couldn't visualize. I asked her if she was planning to attend my workshop the next day, to which she responded, "yes ".

"Do you know where it will be held?" I asked her. "Right here in the same room, isn't it?", she replied.

"Yes. So how will you find it?" I asked. "Will you need to ask anyone how to find it, or will you rely on images stored in your memory of where you were today to find this same room tomorrow?"

That is when she realized that she does in fact visualize habitually. Visual information is stored mainly in nonverbal images without remembering a specific label or room number. This lady will still know that the room is on the main floor, through the lobby, and to the right. She will have an image in her mind as to the approximate size and shape of the room, so it will look familiar to her the next time she sees it. By becoming more aware of her natural visualizing ability and practicing it, she can improve on something she does all the time.

We would be considered dysfunctional if we were unable to recall simple images without too much trouble. Everyone visualizes constantly; we just don't recognize this process for what it is.

Practice taking photographs in your mind's eye of people, places and events. Think in terms of being able to tell a story to someone using those images that you have "photographed." Every time you practice this, the story becomes clearer to the outside observer. More importantly, it also becomes much clearer to you. Imagine someone grating their nails on a chalkboard ….I bet you have shivers up and down your spine with just the THOUGHT of it!

See yourself living your own personal shocking event, such as skydiving if you are afraid of heights. Feel the fear!!

Imagine that you are in a tropical paradise. See the sun shimmering on the horizon; hear the waves crashing; feel the soft sand on your bare feet; smell the salt air in the breeze; taste the cold coconut drink in your hand. When you get proficient at this, your body does not know whether this actually occurred in physical reality, or only in your imagination. In other words, eventually your body responds to your mental images as if they are physically real.

THAT IS THE TRUE POWER OF VISUALIZATION!!!

The next category of strategies for enhancing your visualization skills (the following five points) are reminders of issues I raised earlier regarding global changes in your life. Implementing these suggestions will not only increase your powers of visualization, but will provide a foundation for self-empowerment.

1. KNOW YOURSELF

By guiding your emotions, intuition, and memories of events (both past, present and future) you are fine-tuning your immune system to heal your body. Your mind does have control over every bodily function, so use every tool you have to make all your body systems work for you in the best possible way.

Rather than reacting with old habits to emotional triggers, you will become proactive in the creation of new thoughts and reactions which are healthier. You will be choosing to take in only information that you need to improve your well-being.

Know that you can go beyond any limitations that you may have previously felt based on input from others. Reach confidently toward a new set of expectations of self-empowerment.

Understand that you are responsible for yourself.

To understand yourself better, notice what pushes your buttons. What are your emotional triggers? When you understand this, you can control and then reinvent yourself. When we are in control of our conscious and subconscious selves, we are in control of our immune system and our health.

In your dream state (when meditating or about to fall asleep), synchronize your conscious and subconscious mind through visualization. Let your Intentions and intuitions guide you. TRUST YOURSELF!!!

2. LIFESTYLE ISSUES

Get rid of any obvious poor lifestyle choices, including all of the stress and negativity in your life.

The physical part of this is the easiest. Work less and play more. Spend time with family and friends. Nobody is indispensable at work, but everyone needs fun and relaxation. Everyone needs nurturing human ties.

3. BALANCING LIFE

A basic principle of wellness is achieving BALANCE in all aspects of life - physically, emotionally and spiritually. This is especially important for those who see their path in life as primarily a helping role. Sometimes "giving all" by helping others becomes a highly stressful but invisible burden when, in the process, you have forgotten to take care of yourself. This can be a pitfall for a healer or caregiver as shown in the parable of the alcoholic-turned-healer. Achieving balance is everyone's constant challenge, not just the healer's. When imbalance occurs in any area of our lives, it always teaches us about ourselves.

Balance and counter-balance is the ever-changing dance of life. There aren't any specific guidelines for this since our challenges are very individual. Dance lessons can teach you basic steps, but ultimately it is the FEELING of enjoying the music, developing self-confidence, and letting go of inhibitions which enable you to just DO IT!

4. BE POSITIVE

Surround yourself with positive, like-minded people. Concentrate on what you enjoy. With circumstances you cannot change, learn to change your attitude. Find an aspect about the situation for which you can be grateful and dwell on that.

Monitor self-talk to ensure that what you are telling yourself is positive and reflects your personal goal of wellness. Your expected outcome must be synchronized with your goal.

Do You Really Expect Your Goal To Manifest?

Remember:
Self-talk Is 24-7. You Are The Most Influential Person In Your Life!!!

WEED OUT THE NEGATIVE FEEDBACK AND RE-PLACE IT WITH WHATEVER YOU NEED TO RECREATE YOUR POSITIVE REALITY.

All day and all night, we listen to our own judgmental opinions of ourselves.

RETIRE FROM THE EXHAUSTING POSITION OF BE-ING YOUR OWN JUDGE AND JURY – AND THE JUDGE AND JURY OF OTHERS.

Give others - and ultimately yourself - the benefit of the doubt and move on. How could we possibly expect to judge another's thoughts, words and actions when it is often difficult to assess our own?

FORGIVE those around you, and with that you will forgive yourself and be free to grow.

Leave your personal baggage of anger and fear issues behind you and move forward.

FORGIVE, and then FORGET!
RELAX AND GO WITH IT!!
YOU WILL ULTIMATELY ACHIEVE WHAT
YOU DESIRE!!!

5. KEEP IT SIMPLE

In our society, we consider it necessary to consult an expert on almost every aspect of our lives. When faced with baffling calculations, we must see an accountant. We ask a lawyer to explain the true meaning of a string of indecipherable words. When our body is sending us a personal S.O.S. message, we consult a doctor. We have come to believe that whatever the topic, others must know more about ourselves than we do. Furthermore, we have the idea that whatever the situation, it MUST be complicated.

Healing through your own intentions to return to wellness is SIMPLE!!!

Energy flows within each and every one of us.
We just need to provide it with some direction.
There is no right or wrong way to do visualizations.
My suggestions simply help you to focus efficiently.
Whatever works for YOU is the RIGHT way.
It is an individual choice.

THROUGH INTENTION,
YOUR WISH IS YOUR COMMAND!!!
THIS WILL BECOME YOUR REALITY!!!
YOUR INTENTIONS OR THOUGHTS CREATE YOUR
OWN REALITY.
IT SOUNDS TOO SIMPLE TO BE TRUE - BUT IT IS!!!

I will give you some general visualizations to use until your creative juices kick in. Then you will have the FEEL of it and the CONFIDENCE to customize your own visualizations.

Most important is YOUR INTENTION to return to wellness and YOUR KNOWING that it IS POSSIBLE.

The general pattern to wellness is a healthy lifestyle reinforced by positive attitudes and specific visualization techniques:

You BELIEVE that it is POSSIBLE to return to wellness.
You THINK that you CAN be well again.
You KNOW that you WILL return to a healthy state.
You ARE well again.

Visualize yourself in your optimum state of wellness.
HOW are you FEELING?
WHAT are you DOING, THINKING and SAYING?
IMAGINE YOURSELF BEING WELL AND ENJOY IT!!!

9

General Visualizations

Visualization is more than using our sense of sight alone. We should be achieving a realistic FEELING OF ACTUALLY EXPERIENCING the event. That is when we know that we are doing it right!

Mastering the practice of visualization will give you the confidence that you need for self-empowerment. These are resources that we all have at our fingertips; we just have to tap into them.

Think of your new ideal self as your goal. Then learn that you can and you will achieve this goal. Your body has everything it needs to heal itself. Think of all your reasons to stay well and visualize them happening with you in the picture. Setting this goal and visualizing it mentally will lead to your success.

There is always a constant exchange of information between your quantum hologram and your physical body. Visualizations are tools to empower you to take control over this information exchange process. This is how you can direct your immune system to the desired location to maximize health benefits. IT'S THAT SIMPLE!

When you have a chronic problem, your body becomes so accustomed to it that it compensates for it. To put it another way, essentially the body no longer knows about the problem, so it overlooks and ignores it. In short, your immune system doesn't do anything.

Visualizations show your body that there is a problem. Doing visualizations demonstrates to yourself that you are serious about making a change. Maintain the constant intention to make the visualizations work.

Another general principle involves integration and flow of your thoughts. It is very important to synchronize your conscious and subconscious intentions, since the more in harmony the intentions are, the more effective they tend to be. This means that the level of consciousness in which you can verbally say, "I know I can do it" is in harmony with that little subconscious voice which is deep inside you. Your outcome expectation must also be in harmonious agreement with your visualization and intention.

The following general visualizations can be used separately or in conjunction with your own more specific visualizations. These general visualizations will benefit you regardless of the injury or illness. Make sure that you are comfortable when doing them, whether you are sitting, standing or lying down.

General visualizations are dramatic interpretations of how we are going to recreate our wellness. What these lack in specifics, they make up for in dramatic impressions. Put as much realistic sight, sound, and feeling as you can into each visualization, while holding your positive intentions and ultimate goal in mind. Strive to achieve a realistic feeling of actually EXPERI-ENCING the event. That is when you know that you have fully mastered the technique.

You may visualize these images directly on your physical self, or you may project these on a hologram in front of yourself, or both. These may also be done to a hologram of someone else, but not at the same time as you are working on yourself, as the energy gets dispersed, thus diminishing the effect.

These are the stages for self-healing using visualizations:

FORM the image (eventually the hologram) of yourself, or the person you are healing, as described in Chapter 8.

FOCUS on your goal by using visualizations to:

- *EXIT your existing pattern of injury or illness*
- *REBOOT your system through intense visualizations*
- *RESET your system to what is desired*
- *SET your pattern of wellness in place*

You may find it helpful to practice saying the visualization steps out loud. The mere intention of visualizing will make it happen. DON'T JUST SAY YOU WILL TRY: DO IT!!!

I recommend these "UNIVERSAL VISUALIZATIONS":

1) *Fire and/or Ice*
2) *Lightning Bolts*
3) *SEPs (Smart Energy Packets)*
4) *Explosions – (Vibrational ripples)*
5) *Waterfall - Blue liquid light shower. Refreshing, cooling, relaxing, steady rhythm, RESETS THE SYSTEM*

1) FIRE and ICE TEMPERATURE EXTREMES

Intense heat and extreme cold are useful in both nature and our visualizations.

FIRE

The fire visualization is very powerful and is used in the same manner as it functions in nature. It is a renewal force. It destroys the old and allows for fresh, new possibilities in the rebuilding of a new, healthy you.

Fire Visualization

- *Imagine intensely hot flames roaring through your body. The force of the fire rips the problem from its roots.*
- *Focus on the area where the problem exists. Some people find it easier to be totally engulfed in flames.*
- *Feel the heat and see the problem turning to ashes right before your eyes.*
- *Incinerate it and watch it disintegrate. The ash blows away with the wind.*

This is a useful visualization for a tumor or cancer in one or more areas.

SEE the flames
FEEL the heat
HEAR the crackling
SMELL and TASTE the smoke in the air
MAKE IT REAL

Fire Visualization

Another visualization using heat is the WHISTLING KETTLE.

- *Imagine a whistling kettle at the point where you require healing. The steam is released with great, screaming force.*
- *The heat from the steam is a very focused stream of heat.*
- *Allow the circulation of its heat all around the problem areas, and see the energy blockages dissipate.*
- *It may help to have a whistling kettle in the background when you first try this visualization.*

SEE the steam rise
FEEL the heat
HEAR the screaming whistle
SMELL and TASTE the vapors
MAKE IT REAL

Visualizing heat is very useful for any problem, as the excessive heat attracts white blood cells to the area. This is powerful to use when the problem is systemic, such as lymphoma, leukemia or a viral infection, since you can visualize forcing steam through your entire circulatory system.

ICE

This visualization can be used on problems such as tumors. The life force of the problem can be frozen and then shattered.

• Imagine the problem area freezing over.
• See the cold, blue ice form as if liquid nitrogen were flowing over it.
• Visualize this icy image shattering or melting away the problem.

SEE the problem freeze
FEEL the intense cold
HEAR the cracking of the ice
SMELL and TASTE the frigid, pristine air
MAKE IT REAL.

2) LIGHTNING BOLTS

This visualization is very effective for any neurological or pain issue. It seems to overload the nervous system, forcing it to reboot. You can apply this to any area or organ requiring stimulation. Then that part of the body has to start up again fresh and new, as it is reset to its healthy state. THE NEW YOU EMERGES!

- Imagine that a lightning bolt strikes on the top of your head.
- It rips through your body with laser precision, lighting up your entire nervous system.
- All of the synapses of your brain fire off, sending intense pulses of energy down your spine and branching down until they reach the smallest nerve endings.
- In this visualization, lightning does strike the same location again and again.

SEE the intense light of the LIGHTNING BOLT
FEEL the energy ripping through
HEAR its thunder
SMELL and TASTE its electrical charge
MAKE IT REAL

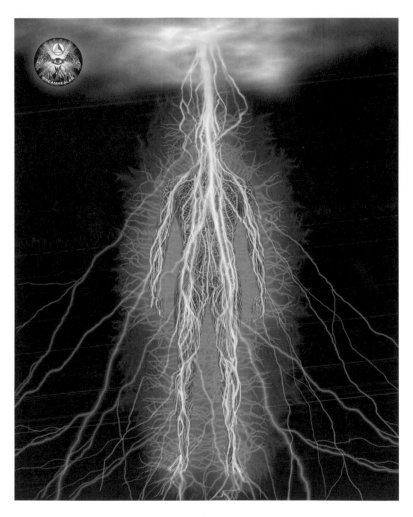

Lightning Bolt Visualization

3) SMART ENERGY PACKETS (SEPs)

Smart Energy Packets, or SEPs are very useful for removing a specific and localized problem. Visualize pacman-like units circulating throughout your problem area. They orbit in a "seek and destroy" mission like swarming bees, yet they spread healing energy in their path.

SEPs orbit and take a bite out of the problem, ingest it, and then eliminate it from your system. It may be easier for you to visualize them as velcro-coated, so as they make contact with the problem, they adhere to it. This stick and remove approach is easy to visualize. Removal is accomplished through exhaling (if it is a lung problem), or elimination of bodily wastes for other issues.

SEPs also reproduce themselves and communicate with each other. This ability is useful, as they can send signals to each other to shock or jump-start the system. They continue to be effective long after you do your visualization.

You may want to make this visualization more realistic by turning the SEPs into white blood cells. Attract them to your area of need. Visualize all of the arteries and blood vessels in your entire body becoming more permeable to white blood cells. This allows and encourages them to surround what needs to be removed from your body.

SEE them orbiting
FEEL them sticking to the problem
HEAR them buzzing as they do their work
SMELL and TASTE the energy they are creating
MAKE IT REAL

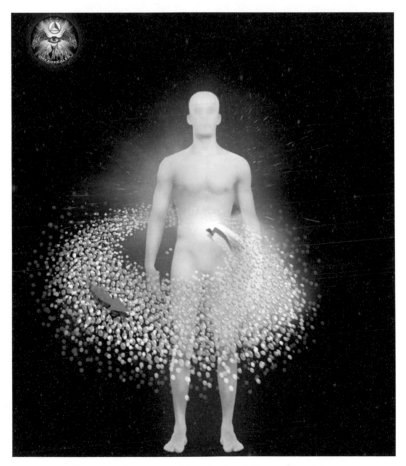

Smart Energy Packets Visualization

4) EXPLOSIONS

This is a very powerful visualization for ripping any problem out of your system.

- Imagine that you are able to blast your problem out of yourself.
- Plant the explosive device right in the center of your problem.
- Visualize this as accurately as possible. Become familiar with the size, shape, or location of your problem.
- Be your own health advocate and do the research required.
- The more detail you know, the more accurately you can visualize this happening.
- The explosion sends ripples out from the epicenter. All fragments are instantly vaporized.

For anyone under 25 years old, imagine playing a computer game where your health problem is the target.

SEE the explosion
FEEL the vibration of the blast
HEAR the boom
SMELL and TASTE the burning matter
MAKE IT REAL

Explosion Visualization

5) WATERFALL

Any of the above visualizations, or your personal adaptations, can be used in any order. It is an individual decision. Try them all and see what works best for you. Do all of them at various times, and you might find that a particular order works well for you.

Use "WATERFALL" last in the sequence of visualizations you choose. This calms, relaxes and cleanses your system. You have visualized the removal of your problem. Now you must repattern or reprogram yourself.

Imagine a shower of blue liquid light energy pouring over and through yourself. It cleanses, refreshes and cools your entire being. Its steady rhythm is soothing and relaxing, and it resets you.

SEE the electric blue liquid light energy
FEEL it flowing through you
HEAR it cascading
SMELL and TASTE its refreshing qualities
MAKE IT REAL

This visualization totally cleanses, filters and purifies you. The intensity of the first visualizations removes energy blocks and allows you to EXIT the pattern of the injury or illness by overloading it. You automatically REBOOT, as this is necessary to RESET the system to your desired pattern of health.

Waterfall Visualization

The final waterfall visualization refreshes and cools. It allows your energy to flow harmoniously in your new patterned energy grid, which can be visualized any time throughout your day. This holds your state of wellness in place.

When you are in your optimum state of health, use the ENERGY GRID to hold it in place. Visualize a three-dimensional grid in the shape of your body. The vertical and horizontal lines are perfectly spaced, or equi-distant apart. All of your energy is flowing rhythmically, smoothly and harmoniously along these lines. HOLD THIS STATE OF WELLNESS!!

This visualization can be done anytime. If you are sitting on a bus or standing in an elevator, constantly practice this visualization. Your mind controls your body, and you control your mind. So work on keeping your mind/body healthy. We all have a perfect blueprint within us of our perfect health. Access it and HOLD IT!!!

How often should you do these visualizations? It really varies from person to person. I give everyone ten minutes in my workshops. Some people can stay longer than that, and if you can, that's great. Whatever you can comfortably do, go for it.

If you find that negative thoughts enter your mind, just stop what you are doing, refocus and redo the visualization. This trains the subconscious to be more aligned with your conscious thoughts.

Visualizations are most effective if you do them just before you go to bed. Keep doing them until you are too tired to continue and then you'll just drift off to sleep with your goals in focus. In your dream state, you are closest to the most effective state of consciousness for healing. You will heal at a phenomenal rate in your sleep.

Your goal is to do these visualizations until you are eventually having dreams about them. This is incredibly effective!

BE A DREAMHEALER!!!

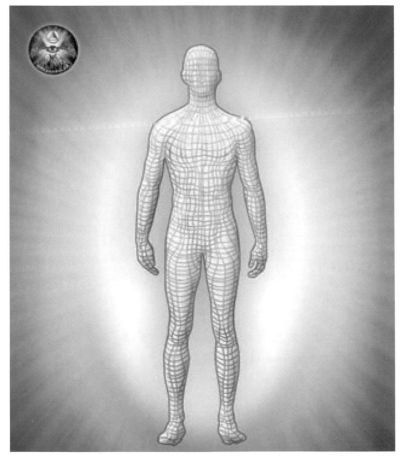

*Energy Grid Visualization Holds your
State of Wellness*

10

Specific Visualizations

Your Doctor should be consulted for any medical conditions noted in this book. These visualizations are NOT meant to replace advice from your health care professional. They can complement any treatment. Whether you use them or not is totally YOUR decision; it is YOUR life...

In this chapter, I will focus on visualizations which I have found to be effective for various conditions:

- Cancer
- Leukemia
- Neurological Conditions
- Respiratory Conditions
- Heart Conditions
- Infectious Diseases
- Pain Issues

- Joint Conditions
- Back Injuries
- Muscle Injuries
- Broken Bones
- Fatigue and Emotional Problems

These visualization strategies incorporate very intensive and detailed information. While these skills are available to all, do not be surprised to discover that they will take a lot of practice before they are mastered.

CANCER

Cancer occurs when cells become abnormal and continue to divide and form more cells, seemingly without order or control. Normally, cells divide to produce more cells only when the body needs them to maintain health. If cells continue to divide when new cells are not needed, a mass of tissue (a growth or tumor) forms.

Malignant tumors are cancerous. They can invade and damage nearby tissues and organs. Cancer cells can break loose from a malignant tumor and travel through the bloodstream or the lymphatic system. This is how cancer can spread from the original tumor to form new tumors in other parts of the body.

Cancer usually develops gradually and is affected by factors related to environment, lifestyle, and heredity. We can consciously diminish risk factors since many cancers are related to smoking, diet, and exposure to carcinogens in the environment.

Some people are more sensitive than others to these risk factors. Inherited risk factors are unavoidable. We should be aware of them but know that not everyone with a particular risk for cancer actually gets the disease; in fact, most do not.

You can reduce your cancer risk by making some simple food choices. Eat a well-balanced diet made up of foods that are high in fiber, vitamins, and minerals. Eliminate as many fatty foods from your diet as possible. Eat five servings of fruits and vegetables each day and lots of whole grain breads and cereals.

Early on in my healing work, I observed some very interesting facts about cancer. I noticed that the cancer cells communicate amongst each other. Cancer is able to replicate so quickly by using a sophisticated communication system.

This can also be used as a tool against its replication and for its destruction. When I did visualizations to break down its communications, a chain reaction occurred. The cancerous cells passed on the message to all the cells in the tumor. This created a domino effect that was very effective in creating disorganization and disharmony within the cells of the tumor. I noticed that creating cell disorganization was more difficult when there were multiple tumors. It was almost as if the other tumors were warned by the tumor I was working on that something was wrong - and to be on their guard.

I observed that as cancer begins to die, this communication between cancer cells slows down and eventually stops.

When doing visualizations for any tumor, the goal is to weaken it and direct the immune system towards the tumor. Your body has more than enough white blood cells to tackle any problem.

I find that the most effective method of getting at the cancer is by attacking it from as many angles as possible. This is accomplished through the use of visualization techniques (based on your own research) and by addressing lifestyle issues, including stress, attitudes, emotions, diet and exercise and your social environment.

Many people have difficulty visualizing without precise instructions. I want to emphasize that there is NO wrong way to do these visualizations. You can use all of the visualizations below, or you can use the ones you feel work best for you, or you can create your own. It is up to you to try these various approaches and observe which ones are most effective for your situation. I would simply suggest including certain anatomical facts which pinpoint the problem for your immune system. For example, an essential visualization for cancer is imagining the attraction of white blood cells to the region of the tumor. The most effective way to attract white blood cells to this area is as follows:

- Imagine all the blood vessels in the vicinity of the tumor becoming more permeable to white blood cells. Allow white blood cells to exit the blood vessel walls and surround the tumor.

- Visualize EVERY white blood cell in your entire body being drawn to the tumor. Eventually, there should be so many white blood cells surrounding the tumor that they form a colony around it, completely engulfing it.
- See the white blood cells that surround the tumor eating away at it. The white blood cells essentially grab the cancer cells, pull the cells inside them, and then digest the cancer.
- Visualize the white blood cells releasing substances which are poisonous to the cancer. See the tumor shriveling up from the toxins being released and from the white blood cells eating away at the tumor. (Note how detailed and physiologically precise these visualizations are.)

The rate at which the white blood cells pick away at the cancer can vary a lot. One variance is the temperature. The cells will eat away at the cancer at a far faster rate in warmer conditions. Therefore, you can also visualize flames raging underneath the tumor to apply heat to the area. Heat increases the blood circulation, which speeds up the healing process.

Tumor

Tumor Surrounded by White Blood Cells

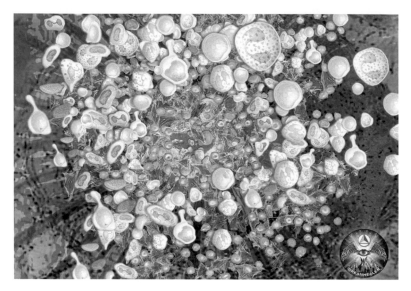

Tumor Being Destroyed

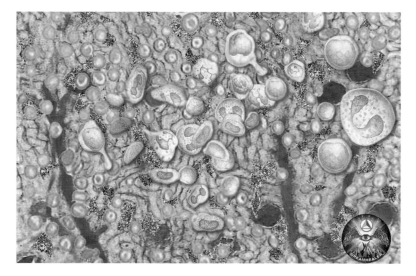

Normal Cells Prevail

A tumor needs nutrients to survive. Without a supply of fresh nutrients and without an exit mechanism for wastes, the tumor will die. Visualize the blood vessels which supply nutrients to the tumor contracting to the point where there is NO transfer of nutrients. Then visualize the tumor drowning in its own toxins and waste products. See this happen until the cancer cells simply die.

Visualize choking off what the cancer needs and simultaneously attacking it in order to weaken the cancer.

As the essential needs of the cancer are being blocked, visualize the communication links between cells in the tumor (or between tumors) falling apart. Once the communication links fail, visualize the cancer shrinking and losing its life energy as it becomes inactive. Your body must now physically remove this tissue. Visualize a garbage disposal system working away 24/7 to remove the physical mass from your body.

LEUKEMIA

Leukemia is a cancer of blood cells, which are formed in the bone marrow.

The goal of any visualization for leukemia is to stimulate the bone marrow into producing a normal amount of red and white blood cells. Visualize lightning bolts going through the bone marrow one after the other until you can see a healthy number of red and white blood cells being formed. Keep doing this visualization until you are confident in this process.

NEUROLOGICAL CONDITIONS

Some of the physical disorders which are neurologically based are: multiple sclerosis (MS), chronic fatigue syndrome (CFS), fibromyalgia (FM), head and spine traumas, central nervous system (CNS) infections and growths, and peripheral nerve disorders.

I have held several workshops specific to CFS and FM, with great success. Many participants report that they no longer have these ailments, and many others note significant improvement in their quality of life. (See testimonials.)

Your nervous system has a direct effect on your immune system, therefore virtually every health issue benefits from a positive change in your nervous system. Regardless of the health challenge you are facing, stimulating your nervous system will benefit you, whether it is an emotional or physical problem.

- Visualize lightning bolts ripping through your entire nervous system. Remember that the goal of these lightning bolts is to "reboot " your nervous system.
- Watch these bolts light up your entire nervous system, from your head, down your spine and to every nerve ending. After this "storm" passes, imagine calming ripples being emitted from your entire nervous system.

I have also found this visualization to be very effective for any emotional or psychological issue. It is also useful in regaining physical energy, vitality and strength.

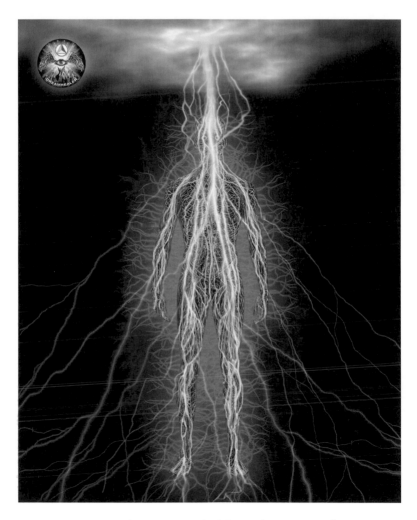

*Use Lightning Bolt Visualizations for
Neurological Conditions*

RESPIRATORY CONDITIONS

There are many conditions which lead to breathing problems. Some issues affect the air passages (such as asthma), while others directly influence the function of the lungs (such as lung cancer).

Asthma is a condition that makes it more difficult for you to breathe. When you inhale, air passes down to your lungs through tubes called bronchi. A person with asthma has sensitive breathing tubes, which may tighten or become inflamed.

Factors which can trigger asthma attacks are smoke, dust, pollen, air pollution, or various allergies. Stress can make asthma worse. To me, asthma looks like a thick, sticky fog throughout the tubes leading to the lungs. Lung problems often respond well to visualizations because there is so much circulation throughout the respiratory system.

With this large amount of circulation in the lungs, the problem can exit the body quite rapidly. Most people with lung problems cough up a lot of phlegm after the treatments. The differences are noticeable very quickly with many breathing problems.

SEPs (images on following page) are helpful, as they can be breathed in directly to your problem site, stick to it like glue, and be eliminated on exhalation. To enhance the realism of the visualizations, feel the problem moving out of your lungs with every breath.

Inhaling SEPs

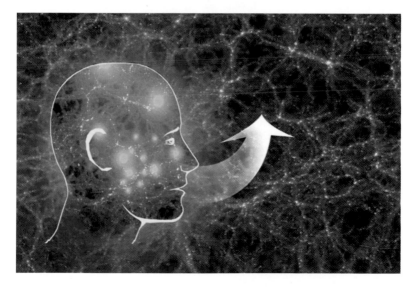

Exhaling SEPs with Debris

Imagine bluish liquid energy filling up your lungs. If you have asthma, visualize your "breathing tubes" expanding as they soak up this liquid energy. Watch your tubes expand, just as a sponge does when it soaks up liquid. The problem is absorbed into this liquid, which then evaporates into glowing energy. Take deep breaths and absorb all of this energy as deeply as you can.

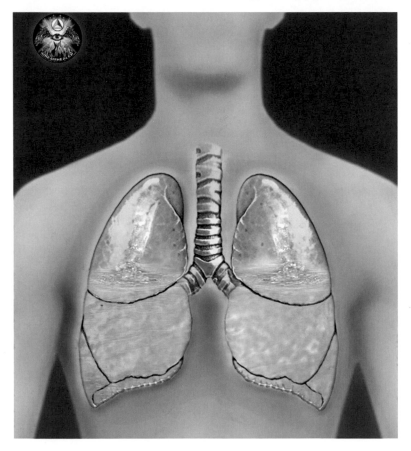

Lungs Soaking up Liquid Energy and Expanding

Visualize a raging bonfire with flames burning underneath your lungs. See your problem shrivel up like a prune, with the intense heat vaporizing it into smoke. Once your problem is completely vaporized, begin to take deep breaths.

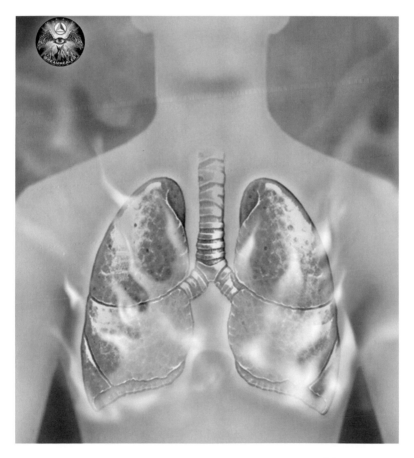

A Raging Fire Vaporizing your Problem

- Imagine taking a deep breath of energized air into your lungs. This energy is absorbed down to the cellular level. See your smallest capillaries light up and reflect this energetic boost. Every airway is clear and bright.
- On exhalation, watch more and more of the vapor leave your lungs until they are perfectly clean and have a "pinkish" color.

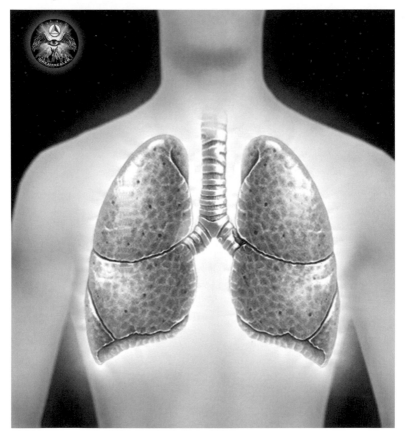

Perfectly Clean, Pinkish Lungs

HEART CONDITIONS

There are many different conditions that can affect your heart, so the first thing to do is to see your doctor. Then these visualizations can be done to complement any therapy, and you can modify them for your exact problem. Remember - there is no wrong way to do these visualizations. I am simply suggesting that you modify them to fit your diagnosis and therefore find what works best for YOU.

Any heart problem is reflected in your breathing, which must be addressed.

- Imagine breathing in pure, fresh air so deeply into your lungs that it energizes the very functions of your cells.
- Visualize this cellular impact of pure energy being absorbed by every fiber of yourself. See every pathway being energized as all cells in your body bathe in this pure energy.

Blood Pressure Problems
(Hypertensive or Hypotensive)

- Visualize your heart filling up with a calming, pure, glowing energy.
- Once your heart is full, watch the glowing energy get distributed more and more evenly throughout your body with every heartbeat. Watch the glowing energy spread down every artery and every vein until your entire circulatory system is completely filled with this calming energy. Every tiny capillary is energized.

- Watch your heart rhythmically pumping, until your heart beat is calm, relaxed and regular.
- BREATHE DEEPLY, and enjoy feeling good!

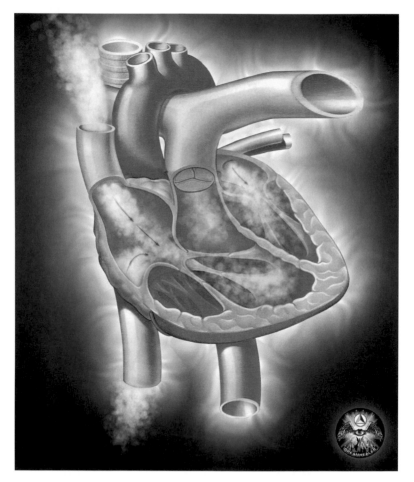

Heart Filled with Calm, Glowing Energy

When using your own visualizations, be creative! The last segment of each visualization with your heart should always show it beating at a relaxed, yet steady rate. With each beat, feel the force behind each regular contraction of the heart.

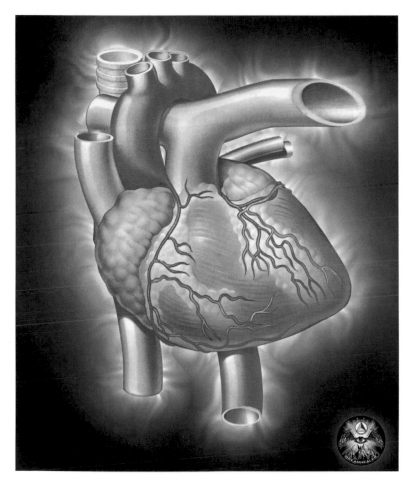

Heart Beating at a Relaxed, Steady Rate

INFECTIOUS DISEASES
(Including AIDS, HIV, Hepatitis, Colds and Flu)

- These type of infections are spread throughout the entire body.
- Visualize white blood cells, or SEPs, dispersing themselves throughout your entire body, engulfing the problem (bacteria or virus) cell by cell.

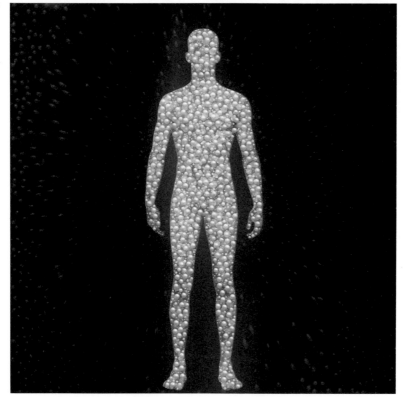

SEPs Dispersed Throughout your Body

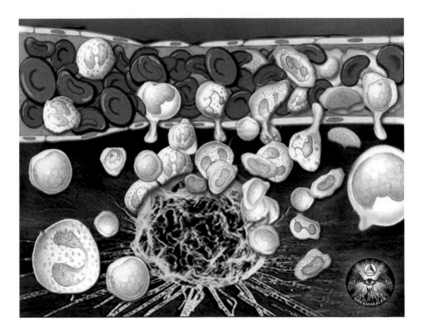

White Blood Cell Visualization

Visualize white blood cells permeating the blood vessel walls in great numbers, totally engulfing a localized problem area.

Visualize explosions in a specific area to address any localized problems. Think of comets or asteroids hitting where it is needed.

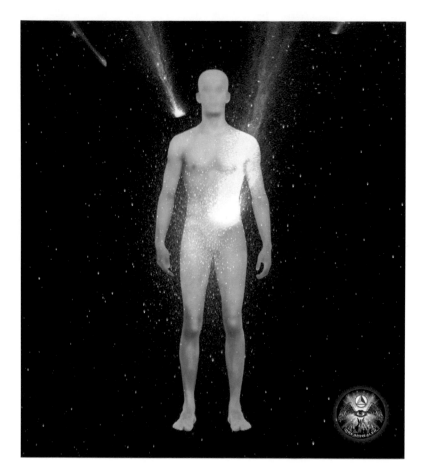

Explosions in a Localized Area

Visualize your kidneys filtering everything out of the dirty blood, or blood which contains the now inactive bacteria or viruses. Continue the visualization until only clean blood is going in and coming out of your kidneys, and white blood cells no longer have anything to "eat."

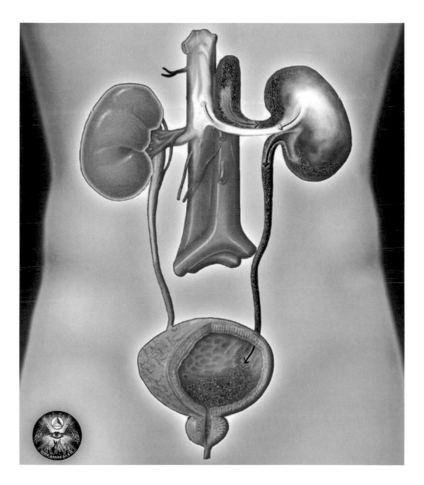

Kidney Visualization

GASTROINTESTINAL ISSUES

Visualize pure light energy being absorbed all along your digestive tract. See the unobstructed flow through your body from your mouth, esophagus, stomach, small intestine, large intestine, colon, and flushing out as waste. See the entire digestive system working perfectly. Calming ripples of energy radiate throughout your system, nourishing every cell in its path.

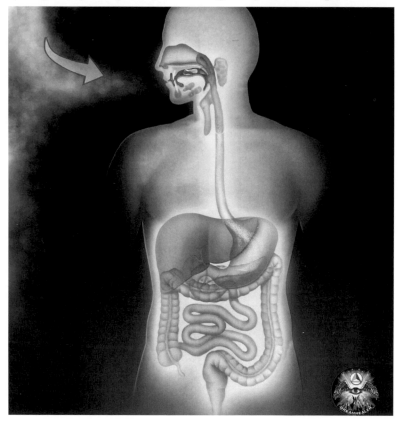

Pure Energy Absorbed Along Digestive Tract

PAIN ISSUES

There are as many different causes of pain as there are people living with it. Typically, mainstream medicine manages pain issues with drugs rather than getting to the root cause. Visualizations vary depending on the source of the pain.

- Imagine breathing in pure, warm sunshine energy deep within your lungs and heart area.
- Form a concentrated ball of energy in the painful area. Visualize this ball picking up pieces of "pain" like lint and then radiating it out of your body in the form of sunshine. The warm rays carry with them everything that needs to leave your body. In its place is left the glowing radiance.

FEELS GOOD, DOESN'T IT?

JOINT CONDITIONS

The following visualizations are for any condition related to joints or mobility problems. Remember, YOU have the power to improvise your own visualizations.

The general visualization using lightning bolts (see Chapter 9) is helpful to many people.

Visualize lightning bolts forcefully moving throughout your joint until it is healed.

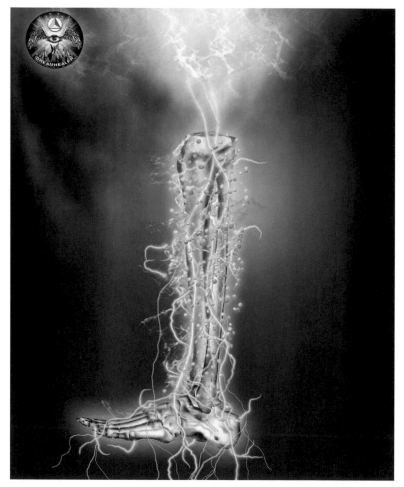

Lightning Bolt Visualization for Joints

Imagine injecting a needle into your joint, dispensing a white liquid energy which totally surrounds all moving parts. This white liquid energy acts as lubrication for your joint.

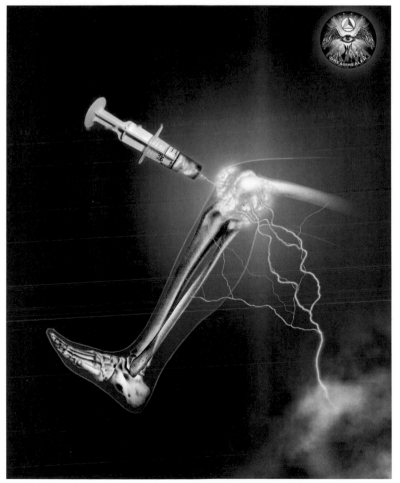

Injection Visualization for Joints

Next, visualize gently testing the mobility of your joint by imagining many support wires at different angles holding your joint in place. Each wire adds support to various parts of your joint, and moves the joint or limb around in the manner of strings on a marionette.

In your mind's eye, test your range of motion by playing a sport you once enjoyed. Remember how wonderful it is to FEEL the breeze against your face as you hike, bike, play tennis or golf, etc.........SMILE!

As the mobility of the joint is being tested (in your mind's eye) there is no pain at all. There is not even the thought of pain present. Remember how this FEELS and recall it often.

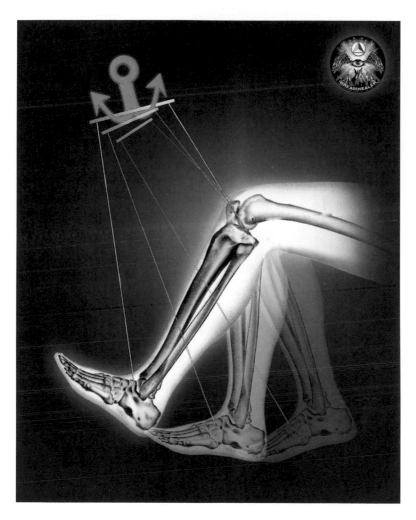

In your "Mind's Eye" Test Range of Motion of Joints, Like a Marionette

BACK INJURIES

- Visualize a glowing, white, malleable rod going through the middle of your spine. This rod acts as a support.
- Imagine that with every inhalation, you are filling your lungs with pure energy. Create an energy flow from the top of your head through your spine and out through your tailbone. Visualize this pathway lighting up like a neon sign.
- Visualize supporting your back while you are moving it around with great flexibility. The range of motion of your back is being tested through your imagery. There should be no painful sensation or even the thought of pain.
- Visualize your back cracking into place as in a chiropractic procedure. Your back is being reset to its optimum position. In your visualization flex your back to test its full range of motion until you have a secure sense of stability.

REACH YOUR COMFORT ZONE!!!

You should then see yourself doing all the normal movements that have not been possible until now because of your back problems. See yourself doing these things with no pain or discomfort whatsoever. What a relief!!

As you experiment with your own visualizations, continue to modify and develop those that work best for you.

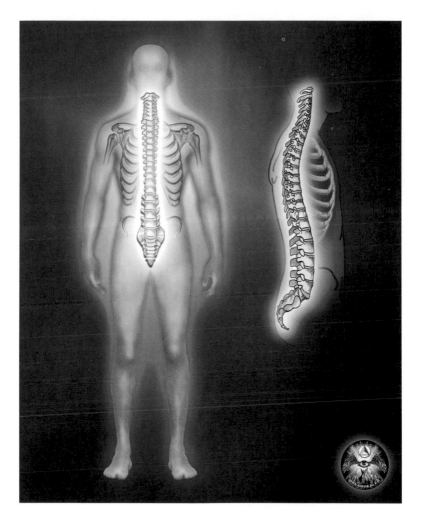

*Visualize a Glowing, White, Malleable Rod
Going Through the Middle of your Spine*

MUSCLE INJURIES

Visualize a calming, white, spiral of liquid energy surrounding the problem area. See all your muscles soak up the liquid like a sponge.

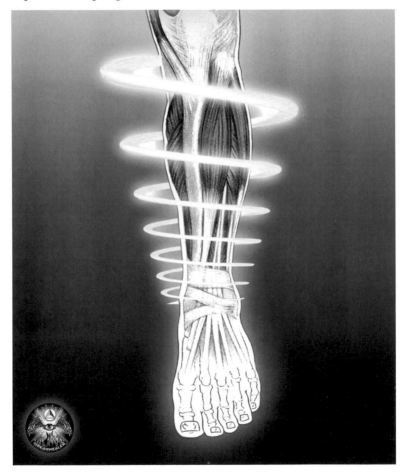

Spiral of Energy Surrounding the Problem

Once your muscles become completely saturated with the white, liquid energy, watch calming waves of electrical pulses ripple out through your muscle. Feel the muscles relax as they bathe in the glowing energy.

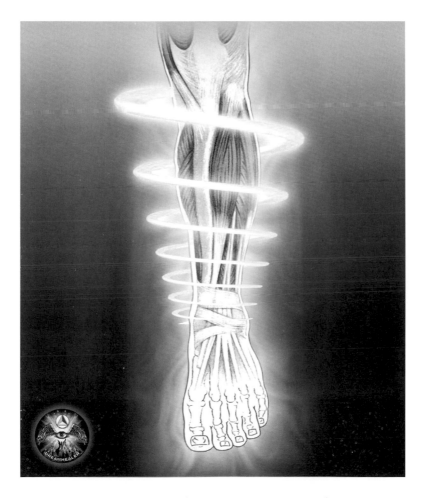

Energy Ripples out From Muscle

BROKEN BONES

Most fractures need to be physically set by a doctor first. These visualizations are intended to speed up your recovery rate.

- Visualize a bright, white light being absorbed into, and then emitted from, the inside of your bone. This bright light creates heat and the heat dramatically increases the rate at which every chemical reaction takes place, allowing an increase in blood circulation. This speeds up the healing process.
- Imagine wrapping energy around your fracture. Watch new, fresh, healthy bone filling in any breaks until there is no longer ANY sign whatsoever of there ever having been a problem. Energy radiates outward as you flood the entire area with warm, healing light to speed up the mending process.

With multiple fractures, you can either do this visualization on one fracture at a time, or you can visualize healing the entire bone at once. Again, use whatever works best for you. There are no firm rules regarding what will work and what will not because any visualization will direct the immune system to some degree.

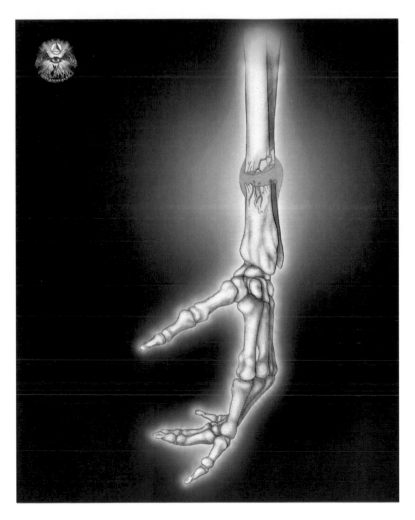

*Absorb Bright, White Light into the
Area of your Fracture*

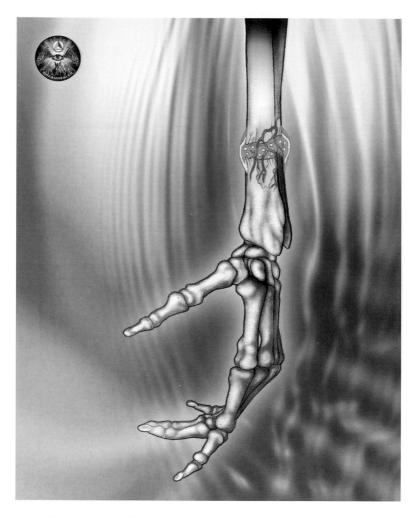

*Energy Radiates Outward as you Flood the
Entire Area with Warm, Healing Light*

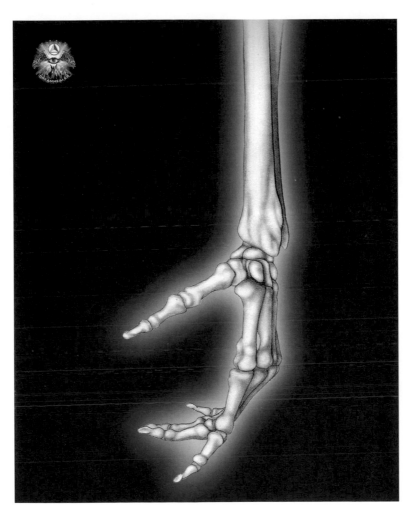

Visualize the Fracture as Completely Healed

FATIGUE and EMOTIONAL PROBLEMS

The visualization for this kind of problem is quite similar to the technique used to expand auras. Do the following visualization whenever you feel exhausted and are in need of an energy booster. I have found this to be a very effective tool in regaining energy after an intense workout. It is also effective in increasing the maximum amount of exercise you can do within your comfort zone. For example, I use this to increase the amount of weight that I can lift when working out in the weight room.

- Visualize all of the energy in the universe being pulled into you. Continue absorbing all of this energy until you feel that your energy system is completely saturated. Doing this takes practice, but it is a very effective skill once you master it.
- Once all of the energy is within you, then imagine that it powerfully explodes out in all directions. The shock wave of energy ripples out. When this has disappeared from sight, all that is left is a perfect, clear, pure white hologram of yourself, with no signs of any problem whatsoever.
- You can also visualize sending streams of laser light to loosen the knot that is holding you back from doing what it is that you want to do. **SET YOURSELF FREE!**

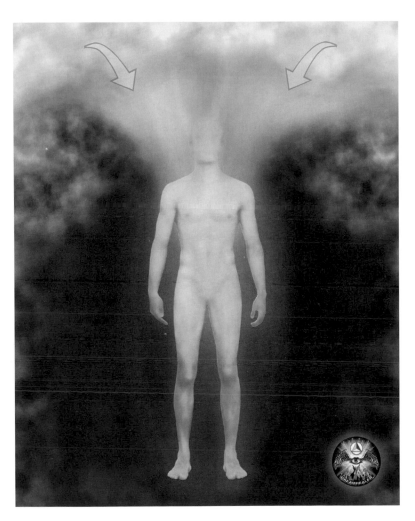

*Visualize all the Energy in the Universe Being
Pulled into you Through the Top of your Head*

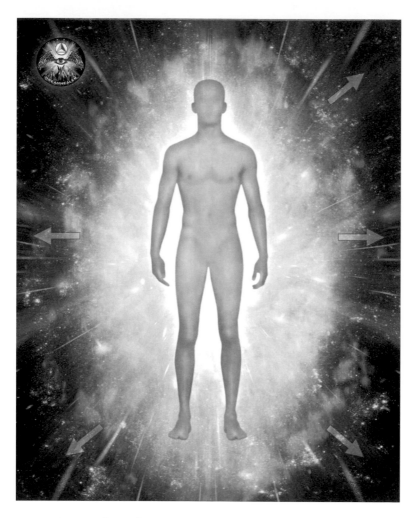

*Your Abundant Energy Explodes Outward
in all Directions*

CLOSING WORDS

If the material in this book has helped even one person with their healing journey, it has in fact helped us all. What appears to separate us is only illusionary. It follows that what we do for ourselves is ultimately what we do for everyone. Helping everyone is therefore an unavoidable outcome of truly helping ourselves.

STAY TUNED!!!

*Any comments you have would be appreciated and can be sent to **comments@dreamhealer.com***

Healing Testimonials

The following is a sampling of testimonials from the many people who have been helped by the workshops. Note the participatory nature of their healing experiences and their continued commitment to practicing visualizations - thereby demonstrating self-empowerment.

I am sitting in my car driving from Toronto to Kitchener thinking about Adam's workshop. I am disappointed that there was no magic light coming down from above. There were no heavenly trumpets or angel choirs. I did not see people throwing away walking canes, no blind people who could suddenly see; nothing like that. Yes, I am disappointed in ME. I guess I have seen too many healing preachers on TV, too many Hollywood movies. I am realizing how much I am influenced by today's instant gratification society. Heal me! I want to see a miracle right now! Right here! If possible, add some fireworks as well...

Suddenly, I feel burning heat in my joints, spreading from the top of my head through my body. ...Finally I am home and so tired that I can hardly wait to get to bed. The next two days I just want to sleep, sleep and sleep..something is happening to my body... my spine is cracking, and suddenly I can bend so easily I can put my socks on without any effort. I can walk down the stairs without holding the hand rails, without feeling pain in my knees. I have so much energy! It is hard to believe that I can do anything I wish without feeling any pain! THANKS....Now can you make me lose some weight??? Seriously, it was an extraordinary experience to feel the results of Adam's healing.

* * *

I just returned from your workshop for fibromyalgia and chronic fatigue. I must say you are an amazing individual and I felt honored in your presence. After the last healing session my pain lessened so much it's unreal. I want to thank you and your God-given powers.

* * *

About a third of the way through your seminar, I heard lyrical, singing choir voices. I can't help thinking the angels were serenading the crowd and Adam. Cool. Maybe another symbol that those up above are happy with your course and how you are proceeding.

* * *

Wow! What a fantastic workshop!! I am so very grateful for the healing that has taken place in my own health - - freeing myself of the painful condition of fibromyalgia. I believe that by using your gifts and special abilities to educate others through your workshops, you in turn will be an influential person making a difference in the world. Your message about the power of intention will help people not only with health but will be used to heal political and environmental problems around the world. I think one day you will join others in history who have made a difference in humanity. I will take pleasure in saying how very fortunate I was to attend some of "Adam's" first public workshops -- and that I was healed!!

* * *

My husband and I were at your workshop, and since then all of my ailments have disappeared. I had arthritis in my knees and high blood pressure. My blood pressure is lower now than it was in my 20's (128/80). I've been running up and down the stairs and on my knees doing all kinds of gardening without any knee pain at all.

* * *

I continue to be impressed with you and your family and the professional yet personal event you hosted yesterday. I have heard many brilliant and well-known speakers, and the comments among my friends who attended the workshop concluded that Adam's articulation and crowd management ranked up there with the best of them. Not only did I leave the workshop with some wonderful tools for working with my clients, family, friends and myself, I left the workshop with such a feeling of gratitude that the future of our planet is in good hands.

* * *

I had 3/4 of my esophagus removed due to a malignant tumor. I could not attend your March 6 workshop; however, my young adult son went on my behalf. He taught me the visualizations, and we were certain that the cancer cells would be destroyed. When the CT scan came back a month later the doctor said, "I don't understand it, but the lymph nodes have actually shrunk." Later that month I went for an endoscopy and samples were taken of the area. The tests came back negative, so I am clear of cancer cells. This is terrific news! Like Adam said at the workshop, there are many things that affect a positive outcome: prayers, medical treatment, support from family and friends, Adam's workshops and his sound advice, our positive attitudes, and of course the self- healing visualizations Adam teaches. Thank you, Adam, for your guidance and amazing abilites.

* * *

During the second group treatment at the workshop, I focused my visualizations on the pain and numbness I've been having in my arms. There was so much energy in the room during the treatment that both of my hands levitated off my knees. The same thing occurred to my feet during the Vancouver workshop in April. It was a very powerful experience. Since the workshops, I've been continuing with the visualizations and have been free from the pain and numbness in my arms.

Healing Testimonials

* * *

Thank you for a most wonderful and inspirational workshop. Today's healing was very profound. I am a Reiki practitioner and will incorporate what I have learned from you today in my distant healing. I look forward to your next book.

* * *

My daughter and I attended your workshop and we both thought it was incredible. I had already read Adam's book and was amazed that he already knew what took me a lifetime to learn. The workshop introduced me to so much additional information with his energy work and visualizations. During one of the healing sessions, I concentrated on my brother, who had shoulder surgery on Thursday of last week and was in a lot of pain. I couldn't 'get' the holographic image but I was able to see/visualize inside his shoulder. (There was definitely something going on there.) The results for him were fantastic. He told a friend of ours Sunday afternoon that he just couldn't believe how much better his shoulder felt than the day before. I got so much from the workshop, but being able to see auras and the energy between my fingers for the first time was a total bonus.

* * *

Adam, to watch you in action is just amazing. You are so candid and fresh, and so yourself. Not holier than thou, not pyscho-new-agey, very science based. If you don't know the answer you say so. Wait patiently folks; coming to a theatre near you!

---

* * *

I have had asthma since I was a child. I felt profound energy during the seminar and my lungs felt as if they were taking full elastic breaths for the first time in many years.

* * *

I AM SO EXCITED. In the first session I was concentrating on my liver. But this morning I found that another problem has been resolved. I have had plugged tear ducts in my left eye for a year now. This morning it appears to be cleared up.

* * *

Raising the energy for the first healing was a new experience for me. I did not feel anything during the healing but afterwards I ached all over.

My back, shoulders, arms, and hands were particularly sore. I felt good but sore – an unusual combination. After the second healing it was even worse. I was exhausted and sore for the remainder of the evening. Since then I have been feeling better and better every day. I have more energy – and a much improved mental attitude. Quite an extraordinary experience.

* * *

I have just returned from your workshop and am looking forward to the next one. My pain is lessening and I can walk up and down the stairs without assistance. The brain fog is gone. What a blessing you are. I haven't felt this good in many years. Words cannot express my gratitude to you.

* * *

It was a pleasure and honor to meet you. I have osteoarthritis and worked on that during the healings. My left hip has been really bad for the last month and I was concerned about attending the workshop because sitting aggravates it. On the way home I realized I didn't have any pain in my hip or anywhere else in my body, for that matter. I thought I would see how it felt when I woke up since the pain is pronounced in the morning. Well..it's Monday – and still NO pain! I have been doing the visualizations each night as you suggested and have every intention of continuing.

* * *

I am from Chicago and traveled to Toronto for the March 6th workshop. I have an autoimmune liver disease which also gives me fibromyalgia-like symptoms. I felt general warmth and tingling during the healing and saw the energy. After the group healing, Adam asked if anyone was feeling any change in their backs, as he had been working on this area. I had not noticed anything there. On Sunday night when I returned home I noticed that there was no ache in my lower back. I had gotten so used to living with the constant bachache that when it disappeared, it took me by surprise. It is now Monday morning and I am still pain free in that area.

* * *

My entire spine feels more limber since the group healing. I will continue to use the techniques that you taught. You have also inspired me to start yoga which should further help my back problem. Thank you for sharing your gift of healing with us.

* * *

Thank you for a wonderful workshop! I am experiencing wonderful relief from lower back pain and am receiving many insights about what I need to do to heal it completely. I have also decided to incorporate your visualizations into my own work as a Reiki master and Kripalu yoga teacher. Everything you said made sense and was confirmation of what I see in my own practice. I had not heard a scientific explanation for distant healing before.

* * *

I was at your work shop and wanted to let you know how much better I felt immediately after the healings. Your book opened my eyes to an entire other side of our lives that we have learned to ignore – and subsequently forgotten about. After your seminar and healing sessions, there was no tension left in my back, neck or shoulders and here it is Tuesday and I still feel great. I have been seeing chiropractors, physiotherapists and masseurs for five years and have never felt as balanced and clear-minded as I do now. The amazing thing is that there was no cracking of bones or deep tissue massage. I want you to know the impact you have had on my life.

* * *

Your workshop yesterday was intensely profound. During the healing sessions while working on my own cancer, I also focused on my uncle in the Netherlands who also has cancer and had just fallen into a coma. He is 80 and has esophagus cancer. This morning (Saturday) I learned that he rallied and come out of the coma. While in the coma, his nurse had told him I was coming to visit. I had not planned to go nor had he had any expectations before the coma of my coming. He opened his eyes, began crying and said my name. The point at which this occurred corresponded with our morning healing group. I now know that I will still have a chance to see him and he will then be able to go peacefully.

* * *

I attended your two-day workshop and I'm still fatigue free!! I still can't believe it. But it is true! I don't remember the last time that I wasn't extremely tired, waking up tired, and going to bed completely exhausted... Thank you!

* * *

Thank you for all that you have taught me. I have read a lot about healers, quantum physics, distant healing, and holographic concepts. But until your workshop, I did not fully appreciate the beautiful gift we all possess. You are going to be a person who will create a global paradigm shift in reference to health and healing and radically accelerate the acceptance of the Mind/Body connection in the medical forum.

* * *

I am a Reiki practitioner and obviously a firm believer in energy healing and the Universal power within all of us. My thanks stem from what your open dialogue has given to my husband. He has had faith in my abilities and those of others, but it wasn't until he saw you on "Health on the Line" (TV show) that he became open to his own. Simply by hearing what you describe of your experiences, he was able to recognize himself. You reached him in 45 minutes in a way that I haven't been able to in 9 years.

****

"I would like to thank everyone for the wonderful testimonials. They definitely give me the incentive and courage to go forward helping as many people as I can - and especially to help people help themselves."

Adam

Order Form

To order further copies of either *DreamHealer* or *DreamHealer 2 - Guide to Self-Empowerment* go to www.dreamhealer.com or use this order form. Otherwise please detach or photocopy this form and mail it with your cheque payable to:

> DreamHealer
> P.O. Box 64121
> Coquitlam BC V3J 7V6
> Canada

Mail/Ship To: (please print)

Name_____

Address_____

_____

Prov/State_____Postal/Zip_____

Country_____

Email_____

Please supply: Amount

Copy(s) DreamHealer - His name is Adam
_____ @ $20.00cnd or $15 (us) each
Add shipping: $4.00cnd or $5.00us or $10us int'l (per book)_____

_____

Copy(s) DreamHealer 2 - Guide to Self Empowerment
_____ @$27.95(cnd) or $22.95(us) each
Add shipping: $4.00cnd or $5.00us or $10us int'l (per book) _____

_____

Copy(s) Both books combined (20% discount)
_____ $38.50(cnd) or $30.50(us) (per 2 books)
Add shipping:$6.00cnd or $7.00us or $14us int'l(per 2 books)_____

_____

Shipping charges listed above are for the first book. For additional books, please add $2.00cnd or $2.00us or $4.00us (Int'l)
Canadian residents please add 7% GST   _____

_____

(Quantity discount available upon request)
                                        TOTAL: _____